PRAISE FOR *BE*

"Herein lie the words of writers who find succor in a leaf, in sixty-ninety-twelve mothers, in data, a sketch, a cold spot, or in the aid of a fireman. The essays in *Becoming Real* infuse the ordinary with the ethereal, reclaiming lakes, liquor stores, leave-takings, and legacies in gulping swallows. These writers dive into life to show readers the spaces in between lived moments."

—Patricia Harrelson, author of *Between Two Women: Conversations about Love & Relationship*

"*Becoming Real: Women Reclaim the Power of the Imagination through Speculative Nonfiction* expands the notion of what memoir can be and do. Narratives about communicating with the dead, communing with the natural world, and shape-shifting as an expression of intense emotion offer readers new ways to understand the mysterious connections that give life dimension. If you're a writer exploring how to express experiences that defy the laws of physics or commonly-held beliefs about what's real, this book is for you."

—Zoe Zolbrod, author of *The Telling*

"Cracking the frame of traditional nonfiction to redefine the truth of living, the speculative work included in *Becoming Real* creates space for the genre to breathe. The ghosts, dreams, fairy tales, and experimental essay forms included in this anthology both inspire and complicate our understanding of what truth in nonfiction can look like—and perhaps, by insisting on the validity of the surreal, how we can better explain ourselves."

—Kristine Langley Mahler, author of *A Calendar is a Snakeskin*

"*Becoming Real* is the perfect gift for your best friends on their birthdays. As we grow older and the world becomes increasingly unhealthy, it is the power of the imagination that will pull us through. From Amy Goldmacher's fantastic scholarly report on communicating with the dead to Gayle Brandeis' tug to return to natal waters to spawn again and everything in between, reading this book is like being taken by the hand of a group of wisdom keepers who have lived long enough to know that the answers are in our own hands. Visionary and empowering in scope, this collection encourages readers to shape their lives in new and inspiring ways."

—Cassie Premo Steele, author of *Beaver Girls*

"The phantasmal and fantastical, woven into the realistic, offer reflection and insight in *Becoming Real*. Discover the power of belief in this wistful, mournful, spiritual, generative, and carefully curated and inclusive collection of women's speculative nonfiction. The power of the mind to hold, haunt, and heal will leave readers spellbound by its magic."

—Deirdre Fagan, author of *Find a Place for Me*

"Who decides what is real? The stories in *Becoming Real* reckon with truth in all its magical, dreamy, otherworldly splendor, a virtuoso tightrope act between fact and fiction, certainty and speculation. These seventeen women writers dare us to witness and remember the gorgeous and the surreal inside our real lives. Yes, they seem to say. Of course it happened that way."

—Nancy Stohlman, author of *After the Rapture* and *Madam Velvet's Cabaret of Oddities*

"A searing, searching, and expansive collection, by turns heartbreaking and illuminating. There is something fierce and crucial in the act of women writing and re-writing their selves and lives before our very eyes."

—Lindsay Lerman, author of *I'm From Nowhere* and *What Are You*

GIRLS WRITE NOW

Fifty precent of net proceeds from the sale of this work benefit Girls Write Now.

Girls Write Now is a nonprofit that serves a culturally and educationally diverse community of women-identifying, trans* and gender-expansive youth and young adults (mentees)—90% of color, 90% high need, 75% immigrant or first generation and 25% LGBTQIA+/gender-expansive.

These young adults, who have long been systemically deprived of resources and opportunities in public schools, face significant challenges to educational and professional success. Unfortunately, in our city and our country, girls and gender-expansive teens of color are rarely given the guidance, care and support they need to gain confidence in their talents and accomplishments, graduate from high school and access viable college or career opportunities, perpetuating cycles of poverty and disempowerment.

Girls Write Now is uniquely positioned to help correct these longstanding inequalities.

To learn more, and to get involved visit https://girlswritenow. org/

BECOMING REAL

WOMEN RECLAIM THE POWER OF THE IMAGINED THROUGH SPECULATIVE NONFICTION

Edited by
Laraine Herring

Pact Press

Published by Pact Presss
An imprint of
Regal House Publishing, LLC
Raleigh, NC 27605
All rights reserved

https://fitzroybooks.com
Printed in the United States of America

ISBN -13 (paperback): 9781646034871
ISBN -13 (epub): 9781646034888
Library of Congress Control Number: 2023950623

Cover images and design by © C. B. Royal
Art on page 111 by Rebecca Fish Ewan

Regal House Publishing, LLC
https://regalhousepublishing.com

Printed in the United States of America

for all our voices

"One need not be a chamber—to be haunted."

—Emily Dickinson

CONTENTS

INTRODUCTION

CLAIM YOUR STORY

Laraine Herring

My first deep relationship with a non-human was with an oak tree in my elementary school playground in Charlotte, North Carolina. I rode my bike to sit in the bowl of her roots and read my books and watch the clouds. This tree spoke to me—not in English but in a deeper, visual language. In this way, she told me of her life and what her tree-being saw and knew.

I learned very quickly it wasn't safe to talk about this relationship. It was not real. I made it up. I made *her* up. I got "lost in my imagination"—a quick path to ostracization, so I learned the importance of keeping those kinds of communications close. I needed to protect myself and the tree.

When I saw my first ghost, I already knew to stay silent. When a house spoke to me in loud, declarative sentences, I listened, but kept it inside. When dreams stretched into awake-time, I watched and sometimes spoke to the elements of the dream, sometimes held their hands or drank what they offered, and always told no one.

When I wrote my memoir, *A Constellation of Ghosts: A Speculative Memoir with Ravens*, I used the term "speculative memoir" because I found no other term more accurately spoke about the way I experienced the story of unresolved grief over my father's death in 1987. The memoir needed the speculative—the talking raven—to tell the whole story—to be the most honest.

I'm often asked for a definition of speculative memoir, and I'm at a loss because all I know is *my* speculative memoir and my experience, and the last thing I want to do is put my own fence around a form that can be and do so many things. So I answer, "To me, speculative memoir is an umbrella genre in which the questions of the memoirist's book are addressed through speculative elements, which may include ghosts, metaphors, what ifs, imaginative scenarios, and fantasies." But don't quote me on that. The whole point of this anthology is to broaden the conversation, not limit it through my own blinders.

I encourage you to ask yourselves these questions: What could speculative nonfiction mean in your creative work? Do you think we all utilize imagination to impact the external world? Do we replay the past, envision the future, connect with our dead and our dreams? And do those actions and imaginings have ripple effects in what we can quantifiably see and share? And finally, how much of what is considered "real" or "unreal" is filtered through a hegemonical system of rigid and binary definitions?

I have seen how the imagination has deep, concrete, and measurable impact on our external worlds. When we can give agency to our what ifs and never weres, conflicts and conversations, ancestors and yet-to-be-borns, those things can provide great insight into our present life. They can help us.

I understand the pushback against pairing "speculative" with nonfiction and memoir. Early in our lives, many of us have been taught to discount the imagined, perhaps better articulated as the things not yet readily explained with the tools we currently have through the lenses in which we've been acculturated. Germ theory was once speculative. Space travel. Artificial Intelligence. Whereas I understand that a society functions best when it can agree on a series of basic facts, the ways in which each of us might relate to those facts and to the world we all inhabit are part of the differences that we should celebrate, not relegate to a far-off corner of literal and metaphorical shelves. Speculative nonfiction celebrates diversity, recognizing experiences that are outside the rational, neurotypical, Western framework, and embraces a much wider, deeper, and richer lived experience. I'm thrilled that speculative nonfiction is becoming more accepted under the umbrella of creative nonfiction, but as long as people have been sharing stories, the form has been used.

Perhaps the pushback against speculative memoir and nonfiction has to do in part with resistance to recognizing the interconnectedness of objects, animals, plants, people, water, earth, and emotions. Perhaps our Western attachment to individualism and separateness makes it harder to *feel* into the places where the unexplained live.

When considering the usefulness of a term like "speculative nonfiction," it's worth considering who made up the rules about what was true and what was not true. Whose experiences count the most? If an experience can't be explained, who declared it inexplicable? In what language? What religion? What nation? What culture? What level of physical ability? There are so many ways to be a human and make meaning of our environments, our families, and ourselves.

This dismissal of lived experience is especially apparent within marginalized groups. Karrie Higgins (they/she), a nonbinary, neurodivergent, disabled writer and intermedia artist, created an online magazine in 2003, championing speculative nonfiction as disability poetics—not a genre or a device, but a lived experience. Their work was met with fierce resistance from the then-gatekeepers of creative nonfiction. Her lived experience was so different from theirs that it could not possibly be "true," but their pushback to her work is not about a failure of truth. It's a failure of the gatekeepers' empathy and imaginations.

Native American worldviews have been dismissed, appropriated, and misunderstood by readers outside of those cultures. As Elissa Washuta, member of the Cowlitz tribe and author of *White Magic* says in "Speculative Nonfiction: A Composite Interpretation", published in the April 2020 issue of the *AWP Writer's Chronicle*, "Indigenous knowledges are often characterized as 'myths' or 'superstitions,' and embodied intuition can be discounted as 'hysteria.' The existence of telepathy is dismissed because of confirmation bias. For many of us, subscribing to a variety of belief systems, the supernatural is, in fact, natural. We speak to the dead. We receive cures from spiritual sickness and protection from harm through developing relationships with non-human beings."

When I proposed this anthology, I wanted to make a space for more writers to feel like the way they related to the world was *true* and *real*. I wanted to create a space where their stories were accepted as written, without editorial interference questioning the veracity of what they had wrestled to the page. I hope I've done that. This is the most profound gift of stories—a chance to step into the experiences of others—and in the sharing of that sacred space on the page, our own minds and hearts open, increasing our respect and empathy for ways of being that are different from our own.

As I considered the submissions, these questions mattered most: How does this piece of writing make me feel? How did it expand my heart? What did it reconnect me to? What did it reveal to me about myself?

Below are additional examples of speculative nonfiction and memoir that have moved me and many other readers.

In 2021, Boudicca Press released *Disturbing the Body: Speculative Memoir about Disrupted Bodies*, an anthology edited by Nici West of twelve speculative autobiographies from women exploring what it means to live in their disrupted bodies. Anna Joy Springer's illustrated fabulist memoir, *The Vicious Red Relic, Love*, is a trauma memoir about losing her lover to AIDS. I would call Carole Maso's wildly innovative 1990 work, *The Art Lover*, speculative memoir, but it was labeled fiction at the time. Piper J. Daniels' 2018 book, *Ladies Lazarus*, is both haunted and speculative.

African-American author and historian Saidiya Hartman's speculative nonfiction book, *Wayward Lives, Beautiful Experiments: Intimate Histories of Social Upheaval*, imagines the hopes, dreams, and lives of Black girls and women from the Reconstruction period. Using what information she found about each subject in historical records, she then imagined the subjects' voices based off her own deep knowledge of that period's history.

Finally, Amy Tan's book, *Where the Past Begins: Memory and Imagination*, is not only a guide to the creative process, but an exploration of how our imaginations are used to help us make sense of our lives.

Like all lists, the above titles are only a small window into a vast and exciting storytelling form. I hope they'll inspire you to find more stories, more authors, more ways of expanding your worldview.

Becoming Real is divided into loose sections. In Part One, "Searches," the writers explore their relationship to their dead or absent family or friends. Part Two, "Interventions," reflects writers who attempt to interrupt or make sense of a challenging experience or person; and Part Three, "Reclamations," illustrates writers coming back into their power.

The essays reflect themes of loss, toxic and abusive relationships, and ways of claiming personal power. The speculative *helps* the writer and makes space for them to grow. In some of the essays, the speculative reflects the literal lived experience of the author. In all the pieces, the speculative allows the writer to move deeper into mysterious parts of themselves and share those places with others.

This is a small collection—seventeen women—and it is not intended to be the defining anthology of all things speculative. It is, I hope, seventeen voices that expand your hearts a bit. Seventeen voices who, through the sharing of their worlds' words, help make your own world richer. You can read the essays in any order you like. Step in and out of the doors the writers opened for you. May you travel safely there and back, and when you return, may you have more space, more curiosity, and more compassion.

Maybe you'll even write your own contribution to the conversation. If you're up for it, here are some questions to help you start your story: What moment, relationship, or place haunts you? What is the one way you have made sense of your lived experience that feels uniquely yours? Tell us, using your unique lens. The more lenses we have access to, the richer the picture will be.

Speculative nonfiction is not a fixed category on a dusty shelf. It's *alive*. I hope you'll join us, and let your story become a part of the chorus of all of us, desperately writing each other home.

PART ONE

SEARCHES

MESSAGES FROM THE PSYCHIC CAPITAL OF THE WORLD: A RESEARCH REPORT

Amy Goldmacher, Ph.D.
Anthropologist at Amy Goldmacher LLC

Abstract
As part of an ongoing inquiry into how reaching the age at which your father died changes how you view him, yourself, and your future, this study attempts to make connection with the dead.

Communicating with the dead presents novel ontological or existential challenges for the anthropologist and raises questions about proof and certainty over instinct and emotion. Using the method of participant observation, or ethnography, this study explores whether a father can still be here, even twenty-eight years after his death.

Keywords: *dead, father, presence, absence, connection*

Introduction
This paper explores whether a father can be here and not here at the same time. By visiting a psychic medium community, practicing mediumship, and having a reading, the anthropologist will both observe and participate in activities to confirm or refute the possibility of communication with her dead father, and look for insight into her relationship with him now that she is forty-eight, the age at which he died.

Data Collection and Analysis
The research was conducted in Cassadaga, Florida, the "Psychic Capital of the World,"[1] from October 7-9, 2021.

[1] https://en.wikipedia.org/wiki/Cassadaga,_Florida

Ethnography, a cornerstone method of anthropology, is a blend of structured observation and immersion that allows the researcher to take part in and collect information from activities in a specific context.

Multiple sources of data provide a holistic understanding of what it is like to communicate with the dead, including:

Mediumship Development Class[2]

In-person psychic medium[3] reading[4]

Find the Spirits After Dark Tour[5]

Findings

This section presents fieldnotes from three data collection events. To provide context, a description of the small town of Cassadaga, Florida, is provided first.

Imagine an intimate community of like-minded spiritualists from New York settling in a camp in between what is now Orlando and Daytona Beach on the cusp of the twentieth century. Today, Cassadaga still has a charming Old Florida feel: old oak trees dripping with Spanish moss, muggy temperatures,

[2] A hands-on, experiential class for all levels, where students practice techniques to strengthen both the psychic and mediumistic abilities.

[3] Everyone has psychic abilities, but not every psychic is a medium. Psychic abilities are sometimes called the "sixth sense," where a person receives information by tuning into vibrational energies. A medium receives, processes, and delivers messages from those who have transitioned from this life to a higher spirit plane. A certified medium/healer has successfully completed an intense study and training program, which may take more than four years to complete. (Psychic tools such as palm reading or tarot cards are not utilized in the Cassadaga Spiritualist Camp.)

[4] A reading, also referred to as "spiritual counseling," is done by a medium who communicates with Spirit to receive messages from those who have died. Mediums strive to present information received in a positive, constructive manner. Therefore, mediums won't tell you bad things or predict death, but rather offer information so that one can use one's free will to enhance or minimize each situation. Assisting you in helping yourself is the medium's goal.

[5] A nighttime guided tour to learn more of the scientific approach to Spiritualism, and how manifestations of Spirit are investigated, analyzed, and classified, including demonstrations of paranormal investigation equipment.

green spaces, a lake, Victorian-style homes, wooden cottages, a sandalwood-scented bookstore doing multiple duties as a welcome center and recreation hall with a sticky front door and bell to announce your arrival, and a cozy, tiny-town atmosphere, due in part to a mere hundred residents making their homes there. It is remarkably peaceful; even a type-A, anxiety-prone, perfectionistic researcher noticed an unusual feeling of well-being and calm upon arrival.

Mediumship Development Class

This weekly meeting in the almost-100-year-old mission revival-style community temple building is open to anyone who wishes to attend. At seven o'clock in the evening on Thursday, October 7, 2021, a dozen people came to the class. Stools and chairs made a circle in the octagonal auditorium, just behind the wooden pews slanting toward a raised stage. After introductions, in which students identified their names, where they lived, and how long they had been coming to the class, we paired up to practice reading each other. I had not done this before, so I paired with the man sitting next to me bearing a remarkable resemblance to an off-duty Santa Claus, who said he had been coming to this class for years.

One partner would do a psychic reading to sense information about living connections of the other person, and then the other partner would take a turn reading. Next, the first partner would do a mediumistic reading to sense information about the dead, and then the other partner would take a turn. (For the purposes of this paper, only the mediumship reading is recounted.)

Santa went first so I could see how it was done. He described a large man who died recently, someone with regrets, who wished he had been closer to me in his life. Santa asked if I recognized this person. Because of his size, remorse, and recency of death, I said it sounded like my father's brother, from whom he was estranged. I found out on Facebook the brother did die recently. My father's brother had tried contacting me a couple of times throughout my life, but I was not comfortable having a relationship with him, given my father's deliberate cutting off of his family.

I told Santa I was hoping to hear from my father. It's easier for those who have been gone for a very long time, over forty years, and those who have recently gone to come through, Santa said; perhaps my father, gone for just under thirty years, hadn't been gone long enough.

Then it was my turn. Despite not having done this before, with little instruction and a fair amount of performance anxiety, I opened my mind. Let feelings come. I sensed a woman, brown hair piled on top of her head, wearing what seemed to be a Victorian dress. She clutched her hands together under her bosom—I made the gesture for Santa. I felt she was out West, that it was dry, there were plains. The more I described, the more vivid the images and feelings became. (Later, back as a group and reviewing how the readings went, the instructor said the more outlandish a feeling you get, the more important to go with it, because you're probably on to something.) Santa thought I was sensing his father's mother, to whom he was close when he was little. She was, he said, very proud of her hands. Though she wasn't Victorian and didn't live out West, he felt I accurately described his long-gone relative.

In-person psychic medium reading
I arranged a private forty-five-minute reading at noon on Friday, October 8. From my hotel just over the town border, I walked the 322 feet to the two-story wood building where sixteen residents lived and worked as healers and mediums in 12' x 14' rooms.

The medium looked just a few years older than me. She invited me to sit in a well-worn floral armchair.

"Please come with the highest and best for Amy. Amen."

There were people here for me, she said. "A petite lady, an elderly woman, very proper and polished, very sophisticated, very simple, very beautiful. She's very well put together. She has sandy blond hair and it's striking how beautiful she is. I mean, oooh girl, if I would have seen her walking down the street, I'd be, like, oh my gosh, she's gorgeous."

This sounded like my mother's mother, with whom I had been very close.

I said, "Can I ask for someone specifically? Is my father available?"

"It's cute... Spirit was showing me a hot air balloon earlier..."

My father took a hot air balloon ride once. I must have been eight years old at the time. He loved anything to do with flying. The ride, a gift from coworkers, meant my mother, brother, and I dropped him off in a cornfield, and watched him rise and float away in a basket suspended under a tent of a balloon. We chased him in our car, waiting for him to descend and return to us.

"...And it's cute because as soon as you said father, I feel leather, brown leather shoes, not like boots, they're like dress shoes... It's almost like I'm about to polish them and I can smell that shoe polish..."

My father worked in the city, and he would leave early in the morning in a business suit, while it was still dark, to start his commute. He was gone a lot, sometimes for days when he traveled for work in sales for Human Resources Information Systems. Often, he would return late, after I was in bed. The sound of his shoes as he walked across our wood floor was the sound of my childhood, alerting me to his comings and goings.

The sound of men's dress shoes on a wood floor had another meaning for me. Before this trip to Cassadaga, my husband had tried on a tuxedo for a friend's wedding, and the sound of him walking across our hardwood floor in his dress shoes triggered the memory of my father, of how closely I watched and listened for his presence or absence.

I monitored my father because his emotions were volatile, often displayed as impatience and anger. Observing him closely was a way to protect myself as a child and to make myself worthy of his love by staying out of his way, by staying beyond reproach. I realized I was doing the same thing as an adult, in my marriage. I was observing and monitoring my husband's moods to anticipate his needs so he would love me.

"…Spirit's very excited about you continuing to grow because you feel like you've been letting go of a lot of things, that from even childhood and even early adulthood you've been kind of going back through those things and really releasing them and not just processing them but actually releasing them."

The sound of dress shoes on a wood floor, a sound made by a man I loved—and anxiously hoped loved me too—connected my past and present.

But did my past and present need to be connected? Did I need to be hypersensitive to my husband's needs and moods the way I had been as a child with my father? Did I still believe I had to earn love? Could it be possible that, as an adult, at nearly forty-eight, I could let go of old behaviors that no longer serve me? Perhaps this study began with the wrong questions.

"…I do feel like you are a medium because you wouldn't have this many spirits hanging around you. There seem to be a lot of them! I believe you have the ability to be a clairvoyant, so believe what you get, that's the biggest thing. Trust what you are getting… It's about trusting in your gift and the information you get."

Trusting feelings was never my strong suit. I had always opted for evidence, for science, for external proof.

Find the Spirits After Dark Tour
This night tour started in the social hall attached to the bookstore. At eight o'clock in the evening on Friday October 8, 2021, two presenters regaled the six who signed up with local stories of paranormal phenomena and demonstrated equipment for spirit communication before taking us out through the community to hunt for spirits.

We took pictures with our phones, trying to capture orbs. We used temperature sensors to find cold spots. We used electromagnetic frequency devices to collect fluctuations in electro-magnetic fields to capture sounds that could be interpreted as voices or words.

Given my father's love of communication technologies, I was surprised he did not take the opportunity to present himself. Surely he knew I was looking for him.

Discussion

My father was remote (ghostly?) while he was alive. Emotionally distant when at home, and physically gone frequently, traveling for work. I loved him, he was my father, but he was troubled. As a child, I didn't know that my father had problems that didn't have to do with me. A child thinks, mistakenly, they are responsible for their parents' happiness. I can see now, as an adult, in a relationship with an adult who has his own baggage that only he is responsible for, I cannot be and I am not responsible for someone else's emotions.

We all have baggage. We all have ghosts.

I am sure my relationship with my father, whose vibration of anger taught me to watch and listen so I could avoid danger and be found worthy, cemented my interest in—and ability to be— an anthropologist, a careful observer, planner, and recorder of information.

Approaching life as a professional researcher is comfortable. More comfortable than acknowledging my ongoing, complicated grief over my relationship with my father. Feeling instead of studying or knowing is new territory for me, a social scientist.

Since he died almost thirty years ago, my father has appeared in my dreams. His words come out of my mouth. I hear his voice in my head. I even received an email from him after his death[6].

---

[6] It was an email I had already received from him before he died, but the email arrived again as a new, unread message in my inbox two years after his death. The message was rather ordinary, a newsy brief email describing the details of a recent couple of days. There was going to be a lunar eclipse, he wrote. It was unlikely he'd be around for the next one, so this was his last chance to see it. I had read it when it first arrived and saved

16

Is he haunting me or am I haunting him?

Conclusions

This investigation attempted to answer the question, "Can a father be simultaneously here and not here?"

I can't say this is not true, based on the data.

A father is emotionally and physically distant while alive. A father dies. A father sometimes makes his way back. As if a loved one were merely away on a business trip or a hot air balloon ride, we wait for their return, or at least a form of communication. Something in us still believes our connection is not broken.

A husband is not a father.

Maybe I should be asking, "How can I find new meaning in my relationship with my long-gone father?" and "How can I enjoy the freedom of not feeling responsible for others' emotions?" Tuning in to and trusting my instincts may open a door just enough for something new to come in.

Researcher's Autobiographical Statement

Amy Goldmacher was twenty years old when her father died from pancreatic cancer, one week after his forty-eighth birthday. Now older than her father ever got to be, she is trying to be open to possibility, to engage with what was lost, and to let go of what's no longer needed.

---

it, knowing that someday soon there no longer would be emails from him. When it arrived again, I decided to take it as a sign that he was still around, maybe as a bit of signal, somewhere in the electronics he loved.

LEAVINGS

Christine Corrigan

My father's ghost lives in my office. Perhaps not a ghost in the hazy, grey spectral sense, but a charcoal sketch of his profile as a young man hangs on the wall. The drawing bears the artist's signature, Julio Viera, and Montmartre, which is where my father must have sat for the sketch. Viera captured my father's mien as I remember him—thick-framed black eyeglasses, wavy black hair, receding hairline, slight grin, narrow nose, and fleshy chin. My dad looks like he's about to tell a terrific story—something he did often.

When I glance at the sketch, I can return to any moment of my life with my dad. I see him sitting with a book in hand and pressed close to his face as he was terribly nearsighted, with his eyeglasses on a nearby table or clamped between his teeth like the cigarettes he smoked. I see him leaning toward a painting at the Metropolitan Museum of Art to take in a particular detail. I see him sitting at our favorite restaurant in Chinatown or at the Oyster Bar in Grand Central Station. I see Daddy at the tiller of his beloved whaleboat, with his eye trained on the horizon. I can hear his laughter fill the room. I can feel his cool hands that I held for the last time thirty years ago—hands that didn't hold mine on my wedding day; hands that never held his grandchildren.

I dwell in his loss and perhaps feel his absence more acutely now that I'm the same age he was when he died. Our days are fleeting—one day, week, month flows into the next and years pass; years without conversations with my dad, years without his advice. I would love to know the story behind the sketch. I wish he had shared it when I was growing up. Did he forget about it in the course of everyday life? At night when the house was quiet, did he pull the sketch out and briefly relive the memories of his trip to Paris?

Who are you really?

From the sketch, I hear your voice as if you were sitting next to me.

Who am I really, Christine? I'm the imperfect man whom you've held close for three decades now. I watch you from the portrait where I linger. I cannot leave this liminal space of graphite and paper. I see you at your desk searching for the words to tell a story you don't know. Sometimes, I slip out—a wisp spiraling overhead and visit the corners of your home where you've hidden pieces of me, well, perhaps not pieces of me, but relics of the second and third degree—things I wore or touched. You have so many, like those collected by pilgrims who stopped at cathedrals and pressed their hands next to sacred bones in search of a miracle or intercession with Divine. These abandoned objects keep me tethered as with so many threads to this middling space. I could call it purgatory but that presupposes prayers would open the pathway to the next world. But all the silent requests for the intercession of the saints will not free me.

I tried to leave on the night of the accident. Then, you walked into the emergency room bay where my body cooled on a gurney. Your mom sent you to identify me, bereft as she was in the waiting room, and not the first time in our family's history where the child has taken on the role of a parent. You did that often, I'm afraid. You stood next to the stretcher and took my hand. I felt—as much as one who's recently departed this life can—you run your fingers over the fine grey and black hairs on the back of my hand as tears fell down your face, but you didn't sob or even breathe. You only nodded to the doctor who then guided you out, but not before you turned one last time to look at me and whisper,

How could you?

In that moment, I knew you questioned the circumstances of my death, whether it was "just an accident" or whether I willingly sent the red Nissan sedan into the oak tree around the corner from home. Whether I did or didn't, the outcome is the same. I am here, and you are there.

Of course, I questioned the cause of your death. No one "accidentally" drives into a tree unless the person had lost consciousness, perhaps from a heart attack or stroke, but the death certificate made no mention of a heart attack or stroke. No other car was involved in the accident. But whether you caused your death or not, you were gone.

Yet, had you lived, you would have left. You'd told me only a few weeks before the accident that you'd found someone else and planned to divorce Mom—twenty-five years of marriage and our family over. I never told Mom what you'd said. Regardless, had you lived and left, you still would have been gone.

I saw you on the day of your funeral, not at the funeral home when the coffin is closed before the Mass, but later at home after the burial. You stood in the doorway of the kitchen. You shimmered and flickered with sun behind you. I could see into the kitchen through you, even though you were wearing your favorite Irish sweater. Then, you were gone. I shouldn't have been surprised by your reappearance and disappearance, though I was at the time. According to various faith traditions, it can take up to forty days for a soul to pass over to the next life. During those forty days, souls may return to their homes, familiar places, and their graves. To prevent wandering souls from getting stuck in this world, Irish Catholic, Jewish, and the Russian Orthodox families often cover mirrors in the home.

I didn't need a mirror to trap you. You left behind so many relics—a ring, rosary, college beer mug, Dictaphone, a briefcase. The word "relic" has its root in the Latin, *relinquere*, to leave behind or abandon. In many ways, I'm one of your relics too. For years, I held on to your Irish sweater so I could smell your aftershave until it finally faded. You gave me your *Black's Law Dictionary* when I went to law school three years before your death, and I schlepped it from office to office over the course of my career, though I never used it. Rather, from time to time, I'd open the dictionary to see your name written in your trademark staccato script. Saying that you wanted me to have them. Mommy gave me your fountain pens, and I used them to sign briefs, position statements, and lawyer's letters. Now they rest empty in my desk.

But the sketch, the sketch. I didn't know about the sketch until after Mommy died ten years after you had. My sister, Jenny, and I found it while cleaning out Mommy's house—a dusty cardboard tube stashed in the back of a closet. When we opened it, we found a perfect likeness of a younger you.

Who am I really, Christine? Before I was your father, I was a young man searching for his purpose. To understand why I went to France, I need to tell you a little about my family.

In 1881, my grandfather, Francis, emigrated from Galway where he was a ship rigger. I imagine this is why I always felt at home near the water or on a boat, just as you do. Eventually, my grandfather settled in Elizabeth, New Jersey, with his wife, my da, and his sister and brothers. When my da was old enough to go to work—probably around 1907 when he was sixteen—he moved to Greenpoint, New York, and got a job as a pit man at the Standard Oil Company of New York. His brothers already worked in the shipping trades. Sometime after my da moved to Greenpoint, he met my mother, got married in 1913, and had my four sisters in quick succession. By the time I arrived years later in 1936, my parents had moved from Brooklyn to Ozone Park in Queens, though my da continued to work at Standard Oil until he dropped dead from a heart attack in 1951. He was only sixty, and I, fifteen.

After my da's death, I had no one to guide me. Of course, my ma tried, but she was a widow and exhausted, having already raised my sisters, who by then were in school or working, married, and starting families of their own. Now and then, my sister Rosemary's husband, Norman, helped with my schoolwork, but mostly, I lost myself in books and imagined a different life. I hated the stink of the oil works that followed my da home. I wanted to go to college, and I went to Paris after I graduated from college in 1958.

৵

Who am I really, Christine? Before I was your father, I traveled with your uncle Norman to France. I was trying to figure out whether to go to law school or pursue my dream of becoming an artist. My mother insisted that Norman accompany me and hoped that Norman would convince me to go to law school. Though I did meet some of my college buddies during my trip, I don't remember why I didn't mention Norman in my travel stories. No matter. During the trip, I visited Notre Dame, as you did decades later, and lit a candle for my da. I walked along the Seine and perused the Bouquinistes' collections and found a book of poetry by Edna St. Vincent Millay, my favorite poet. Do you remember it? I read poems to your mom when we were dating a few years later.

I toured the Eiffel Tower, the Louvre, and the Jeu de Paume, where I spent hours walking among the paintings of France's Impressionists and post-Impressionists. Now, you know why I loved visiting the Impressionist collection at the Metropolitan Museum of Art and why your mom and I took you, your brother, and sister there.

One morning, I got up early to watch the sun rise from the Butte in Montmartre. I climbed the cobbled streets to the Sacré-Cœur Basilica, as the rays washed the white travertine cathedral with gold light. I'd never seen anything so beautiful, so transcendent as that moment. I sat in front of the cathedral and sketched as Montmartre came to life—cafes opened, shops accepted deliveries, and the streets filled with people making their way to work. I quickly sketched the emerging scene. As I finished my drawing, from out of nowhere, a towering bushy-haired, bearded man appeared in front of me and asked to see my sketch pad. As a native New Yorker, I was naturally suspicious, but I handed the bearded Goliath my pad and asked,

But why?

I'm a grand artiste, or will be, and I like to see if I have any competition, the tall man replied and flipped through my sketches.

I don't dare breathe.

Perhaps, this artist will encourage me to pursue my work.

He handed my pad back to me and said,

Your technique is precise, excellent details, realistic renderings mais. . .

But what?

They have no heart, no soul, no emotion from you on these pages.

His words drew the breath from my lungs.

I know.

Your work is very good and if it brings you pleasure to draw, then draw. Why don't you come over to my easel across the square and I'll sketch your portrait?

That's not necessary.

It would be my pleasure, please. I didn't mean to be rude. My name is Julio Viera, he said and extended his hand in greeting.

Marty Shields, I replied and shook Viera's hand.

We walked across the square to Viera's easel. Viera worked quickly using black charcoal pencils, glancing at my profile as his hands flew across the paper. He looked up and down one final time.

Eh voilà. Finis!

I couldn't believe my eyes. Viera captured my essential self in a few strokes of a pencil.

How did you do that? I asked.

When I work, I do not think about what I'm seeing so much as what I can capture from the inside—your intellect and wit that I think you have. That's not to say that I don't believe in figurative drawing. I do. I'm not an abstract artist, but I do try to do more.

Viera signed his name with a flourish and added, *Montmartre. You like it, no?*

Yes, I do. Thank you.

Declining my offer of payment, Viera rolled up the sketch and slid it into a paper tube and handed it to me.

I kept this portrait as a reminder both of the young man I was and of the stinging truth of Viera's words. Although sketching remained a respite for me from life, work, and family, I never wanted to share the portrait because I didn't want to admit that Viera's words fixed my life's path. I returned from France, applied for my first job at Caledonia Hospital (where I met your mom), and eventually attended Brooklyn Law.

I remember you drawing when I was growing up. I used to ask you for help on any school projects. But why didn't you finish law school?

I didn't finish law school because life got in the way. I had a full-time job, was newly married, with a baby—you—on the way. My responsibilities at work were growing, and I didn't want to take what little free time I had away from your mom to study. Truth be told, I never liked law school. But I was so proud of you when you went to law school and pursued a career in law, particularly employment law, since my career centered on human resources.

You and I aren't so different from each other after all, Christine.

True, we're similar in our love for words, books, arguments, and art. We both love to craft and share a good tale. We both hold on to memories. We differ in the most important respect, however. I would never want to leave my children wondering about how and why I died.

What you say is true, Christine.

Who was I really?

I was an imperfect man who's spent three decades, a wrinkle in the universe from where I sit, reliving my mistakes, waiting in the grey, trapped in charcoal and newsprint.

Waiting for you.

❧

I have held you for so long; yet, for all of my holding, I cannot bring you back.

❧

No. You can't.

❧

I gaze at Viera's sketch of my dad as I still remember him—with his thick-framed black eyeglasses, wavy black hair, receding hairline, slight grin, narrow nose, and fleshy chin—and I smile.

❧

I feel a pull, a tug, and I'm free from the frame. Buoyed by your words, I rise above your desk and become the faintest glimmer. I flit through your home acknowledging and leaving the relics you kept—the sketch, the law dictionary, the pens, the rosary, the ring, the mug—bound to them no more.

And as I pass through the window, I find myself soaring above an endless sea. I inhale salt air as I rush toward the horizon, homeward bound.

❧

I turn again to the portrait and notice my dad's raconteur's grin has softened, as if the story he was about to tell has faded from memory. His eyes are small slits behind his thick black glasses, and a thin crack has appeared in the corner of the frame.

A grey heron flies past the trees beyond my window, headed to the pond where she'll spend the season at the edge of land and water. The faintest scent of salt fills the air around me—a whisper, a promise of a life to come.

THE MOTHERS

Leslie Lindsay

In my lifetime, I have had at least *sixty-ninety-twelve* mothers.

The mommy of my early childhood is a ravishing beauty, golden tan, hair pinned back in honey waves. Charismatic; a gleaming smile that could melt ice. This mother could do anything she set her mind to: tailor a suede suit for her mother's friend, refinish a cabinet, paint a canvas. She relished in feeding. Not always herself, mind you. But my father. Me. She lovingly, if not dutifully, stood over the stove, stirring, sautéing, adding cornstarch to gravy. She often taste-tested sauces, dipping the spoon into the skillet for me, the scrape of wood on my baby teeth like a pulse and then retreating the implement with a pleased expression.

This was the mother I yearned to be, the one I wished to emulate. At preschool, with my friends, I would gather them at the play kitchen, where I tended to the miniature oven, make-believing the boy was my husband and the girl, my daughter.

This mother kept an impeccable home. The furniture polished, the drapes open, the vacuum lines uniform. She purchased a blue plastic upright for me, which whirred when pushed, but nothing more, no beater brush, no suction. She gifted me a tiny ironing board that clanged when unfolded, a plastic 'iron,' which I ran over cloth, remnants from her sewing room.

We cleaned and laughed, shimmying in the dust motes to the tunes of Fleetwood Mac and The Beatles.

My mother.

Those days began to shift, edges of disarray crept into the fold. Anger simmered from her pores. Her skin grew sallow, puckered. Her sewing room held the hint of frustration, of half-finished projects, wads of material strewn about, a head-less dress mannequin tipped on its side, oozing brown foam. Everything was 'stupid.' She stomped through the house, chain-smoking Virginia Slims, downing cans of Tab; the knot between her eyes grew tight, a pulsing urgency.

Meals became Triscuits and cheese, summer sausage and Cheetos.

The daughter was an only-child at the time, with a make-be-lieve friend called Jen-Jen, and a doll referred to as Baby Beth.

The first mother stayed behind, at a faux-Tudor two-story on the outskirts of town, when we moved to The Big City. The door was bolted shut, the key lost. The real estate agent grinned as the final paperwork was signed and the United van loaded possessions, slapping blue numbered stickers on our furnishings.

The new house presented cracks and fault lines, a hoard of roaches in the basement, oozing white with sludge. This mother wanted everything pristine and brand-new, a fresh start. She wanted everything she felt she deserved but could no lon-ger have: six-panel doors, brass doorknobs, kickplates and bay windows. She pried the lime-green linoleum from the floors, yanked the blue carpet from the staples, no longer united. This mother lamented that she had no friends and was forced to flee. To flee? The word was wrong, but the feeling all the same.

This mother.

That mother.

She grew tiresome. Weary. Then elated. Her smile burnished itself on windows and walls. Wallpaper got stripped and hung anew. This mother searched for suitable home furnishings then rejected them. Search. Reject. Search. Hang. Reject. Re-hang. Search. Reject. On and on and on.

In the yard, the yard that was never hers because it belonged, in part, to the woman who lived there previously, the one who started it, who arrived long before my mother, in gingham and clamdiggers, whose hair was wrapped in a bandana. This

woman, the previous owner-mother, did things the simple way
with clothes on the line, a plastic pool for the children, pea-
nut butter on white bread. But, no, this was not enough. The
second mother wanted edged flower borders and lush mulch,
rolling waves of green, a custom swing set, a playhouse for the
children. Never mind that she had only one.

Child.

Elusive.

Slipping through like silt.

Here, she tilled the earth in bikini tops and running shorts,
her sweet scent speckled with musk. She planted blue spruce
and geraniums, marigolds, bright with sun. Her skin darkened.
And sometimes, too, her mood.

"Those people," she'd say. "The ones who used to live here."

What did she mean? Her nails would be caked with dirt and
grit, like soiled coffee grounds, eyes lit. The earth became like
an archaeological dig. Pieces of the strangers' lives would surface: a baseball card, a button, a water gun.

She wanted to obliterate that woman, that family from
before. Was it really the previous owners she wanted gone, or
did she feel a dark liquid shadow of something lurking, something she couldn't even discern? Did the second mother feel an
urgency to erase that life? That woman? Did she know?

What do we know now?

That mother.

The roots of origin. The draped window. The shrouded
sewing machine. The hunched mannequin. The heaps of fabric. A velvet darkness, a fuzzy unraveling.

Plink, pluck. The thread was loose.

This mother, the third mother, came with loose bits and
bobs, the jangly, jaunty look of fevered children, tired beyond
tired. She smelled of moss, mold. Veins burbled to the surface, jagged blue lines. Suspended in the sky were layers of her
skin, a swelling possibility of silver, white, gray. And she sat in
her robe, sometimes in blue, and other times, the diaphanous
nightie, the one meant to be sexy, but was worn inappropriately

around the house in the daytime, with the child. The girl who once pushed a plastic vacuum and diapered cloth dolls.

Who wanted to be like

Her mommy.

But now, had to be watchful.

Like a mommy.

This child hunted and cobbled facts, made observations. Watched the clock, the pantry, the door. She listened for the trill of the phone, the shock of outrage.

The fourth mother spoke in riddles and yearnings. Hallowed sighs that simultaneously sounded thrilling and enchanting but also terrifyingly frightening. Her eyes yellowed and bespoke fear and something else: a blazing fire within, charring the architecture of domesticity.

Outside, the flowers wilted. The heads of rabbits were found, moist, blackened feathers. Here, was the margin of a new earth. Of a mother on the brink.

This mother spoke of *missing out*. She worried on watches and clocks, thinking they were lie detectors or bombs. The lamplight was God and provided healing energy. This mother spoke of killing the neighbor and sleeping with the old man across the street. She believed the father was gay or bisexual and ready to divorce her anytime. This mother said she was everlasting love and wanted to redeem the world. She had the power within.

She said she was going to kill the children, that they were the devil.

The father fretted for his daughters. He coaxed them to their rooms, locked the doors, kept them safe. He phoned his wife's mother who said, "It's you. It's your marriage. Deal with it."

In the purpled dawn of day, this mother stumbled along hallways, refusing sleep or clothing. She declined clothing. Pendulous breasts swayed, her lips snarled, like an animal. The urge, the pulse, the need to transfer this mother from the bedroom to the garage, to the car, to the hospital,

like an obliteration.

Of a mother.

Who once tended to the hearth and home.

The liquid echo of tires on asphalt, the screeching of words, the bending of tendons and bones. This mother said, "I'd rather die than go to the hospital."

She went to the hospital.

The third mother transformed into a chimera of sorts, half-woman, half-mother, half-monster, emerging like a sequence of shadows of yesterday, of what used to be.

I and me. You. These are conventions that no longer apply. The mommy of my childhood is dead. There is a dissonance and a detachment. It is what must be done.

To persevere.

At home, the same drapes, the same mirrors, the same floor-boards and paintings. Slowly, insidiously, the home became a battleground, a shell. As her steps grew near, the door opened, something rustled, a remnant of who once had been: Mommy, second mother, third.

And then

the home crumbled to a ruin. That mother disappeared, and yet all was revealed.

Fourth mother grew manipulative and spiteful. Rampant, yet indistinct, she trolled the neighborhood in her car, picking fights with neighbors, mowing over mailboxes, leaving animal excrement on porches. She called incessantly, the phone blaring and beeping, clogging answering machines. Doorbells rang fre-netically, windows covered with blankets. Doors were pressed opened and closed, a membrane of sane and insane, a glimpse within, the swell of possibility, a sliver of home.

In California, this mother shares a bed with her daughter, swelling of salt and sweating psychotropics. The daughter watches as palms rustle against the window outside. Fearful for her future. This mother sighs in the silk peach sheets and mumbles in her sleep. She snorts coke and smokes marijuana and has an unhealthy fascination with sex and death.

The fifth mother loses custody of her daughters. Suspended.

Detained.

Betrayed.

She is visited at the psychiatric ward by her once-blue-plastic-vacuum-doting daughter, who held Baby Beth to her chest and ironed scraps of fabric, who is now a high school senior. This mother is not wearing clothing, but a hospital johnny that will not close in the back. This mother, the sixth mother, is insistent that the daughters have been sexually abused. She shows the daughter her cunt and says, "You came from here."

This mother once believed she was pregnant with the messiah—twins. In actuality, she shoved a lighter in her vagina, in effort to conceal from hospital staff. She urinated in drinking cups, and demanded nurses drink it.

See, nothing?

She pins fabric and sews draperies, clothing. A magic trick transpires.

The seventh mother berates her daughter. She removes a front door from the hinges and claims she has a body guard with gold knuckles. She fears a hit man is after her.

The daughter goes to nursing school. She learns about things, but knew them all along. Psychosis. Narcissism. Bipolar. Schizophrenia. She completes her clinicals at the state hospital where men ejaculate in tubs because they believe it will cure them of the their ails. Women sing songs and stare wide-eyed from windows, into space. And the daughter knows. She's seen it all.

The eighth mother sells everything and flees to a tropical island. The sway of palms, the crash of the ocean do nothing but drive her further to madness. She brandishes a knife on a police officer and shaves her head because it interferes with her creative process. The eighth mother lists her daughter-in-Missouri as next of kin. On a limpid spring day, a packet arrives at the daughter's apartment. A pile of papers: request for involuntary commitment. And then, a week later: persona non-grata.

Locked out. Door slammed.

What do we know?

This mother.

And that mother.

Is tormented with things unseen. Voices and manifestations of a dream from

Long Ago.

She fears things and reaches into the past, which is not the past. And says, "I only wanted to play house, with you, when we sewed and made things." This mother storms about her apartment, hefting sewing machines and tossing silk like confetti.

She holds the keys and barricades the door. Her eyes grow sinister. Opaque. Seeing through, or

Maybe Beyond.

The daughter says she must go. It is late and she must study. But the best specimen is here, within these walls. The *ninth-tenth-eleventh* mother—she's lost count—has a grip on her, like a vice. The mother bares her teeth. "Do you know the way?"

"Of course," the daughter says. She looks at the mother with a mix of sympathy, pity, and fear. In the dark clutter of the mother's kitchen, she decides that the house of her future will be bigger and brighter, with malleable walls, a structure that breathes.

The journey is not easy. Not in the way expected. Who is she if not a woman, a daughter,

of a mother

with a problem?

Who once lugged a plastic vacuum and a water-logged cloth doll? The weight of her childhood. She isn't sure if she can be a writer *and* a mother. She isn't sure if she should be an artist, at all, like her mother.

Isn't a writer an artist?

Nursing school is charts and notes and patients. Clinicals and vitals. It is hustling in the wee hours of the day and starching.

Things white.

And being objective.

It is the opposite

of art.

Of the twelfth-thirteenth-fourteenth-fifteenth mother, the one who says she's dying and "have mercy on my soul." Who says, "You are a woman of science. You must help."

But the daughter knows. She knows.

She knows.

She is a mother herself now.

"No, Mother. You are not dying."

The sixteenth mother hangs up the phone on her daughter. "You are such a bitch."

The daughter visits her father's home. In a room, where her childhood furniture rests, above the kitchen. She can hear the murmurings of day-to-day below, the clang of dishes. With her own daughter, an infant. Who will not sleep, who clings to her chest. Who cries when the daughter-mother places her in the port-a-crib. Pick up, put down, pick up.

The child.

The daughter-mother lowers to the same rocking chair that the first mother once rocked her. She arcs back and forth, spilling milk, dampening her shirt, cradling her crying baby. She has nothing.

She has everything.

A mother is a nurse.

A mother nurses.

If I nurse, I am a mother.

Is this objective or subjective?

The floor shudders

with our weight.

The mother. The original mother—we forget which iteration—seventeenth? eighteenth?—will not tolerate being told what to do or how to do it. The *seventeenth-eighteenth* mother will come to the daughter's house. She will bring a sewing machine. She demands it will not be set up in the basement or a walk-in-closet. But the daughter thinks it best, to have it.

Out of the way.

A closet. A basement, she suggests.

Those are places that protect the home.

From clutter.

Disarray.

From her mother's disorder.

"Absolutely not," the mother says.

The children—two daughters, nearly identical—stare wide-eyed.

The daughter-mother thinks of geometry and order. She remembers her family history, her threads of origin. She recalls her vow: a house of light and space.

She acquiesces.

How many mothers is it now? *Seventeen-eighteen?*

Nineteen.

The age the mother was when the daughter was born.

Colicky baby. Crying mother. Child bride.

Married off. Sent away. Good riddance.

Here we say this:

The mother died.

She was found in her home, where she took too many pills.

Because the daughter was once a nurse, she knows:

The body is a vessel.

She knows of skin slip and bloating and gases. She knows of blood pooling, the way fluids seep. She knows the mother's hair and nails will remain for years, but the eyes,

will do something that resembles Dali's clocks.

The daughter has become a mother. But not that mother.

She hauls out the vacuum. She must clean. Not her mother's home. She will not go back there. That home is locked, should be burned. The wreath askew, the patio stones chipped, like her mother's tooth.

The thirty-sixth mother is one who has a dead mother. The thirty-seventh mother is the one who dwells in the mysteries of her mother's life, who worries, "Will I be like her?"

But the daughter knows.

She is not like her mother at all.

The thirty-eighth mother delves into the medical records, absorbing, with a clinical eye.

The psychopathology,

of her mother.

Will they follow her? The daughters of the daughter of the mother? Those tiny, boisterous bodies she set in motion,

Unknowingly, because

Genetics.

The daughter relishes in knowing she is younger than that tree.

On the banks of the river.

And looks for all the other mothers. The ones she knew were there

All along.

Who send letters in the mail bestowing sweetness and light.

Or the ten hawks circling above, reflected in a ribbon of water.

At her feet.

She finds more mothers smiling at ice cream stands in small towns, handing over ice cones and hot dogs.

To their children.

How many now? Sixty-five or fifty-five?

Twenty-two hawks.

One mother.

Does it matter?

Do we count backward? Or forward. Where do we start? One hundred? One million?

The dome is tipped.

Upside down.

Nurse mothers comfort and laugh. Yoga mothers shapeshift into philosophers and psychologists, comedians, and call you daughter. Other mothers frame antique letters and tell you their story of origin.

Another soothes water over river rocks and drops heavily pigmented leaves from branches. She gusts a breeze from nowhere, and tilts the earth. And sends hawks to soar,

where you write.

Is she the one who sells you carpet and says, "My dear, you did a wonderful job."

The daughter smooths the fibers. She picks up a pen, remembering the toy vacuum of her youth, the uniformity of chaos.

Does the fabric match? Is the blue right? Are the children healthy? She grips a blank sheet of paper.

Trembling, with possibility.

THE SPACE BETWEEN YOU

Malia Márquez

You dump in ground beans. Your spirits jump a little, dance a jig. The coffeemaker burbles signs of life, pours forth the scent of crushed-earth roasted, sweet, dark elixir. You sit together, your friend and you, silently in two chairs set in a spot of sun in the yard. Relief rushes through you as a bitter river of heat runs down your throat.

You are no fool. You believe in boundaries. Not walls, exactly. More like the acequia or arroyo, channels human or nature-made; or perhaps a good old-fashioned barbed-wire fence one can see through but not pass. To the side, to the side, to the side, you wave them by. There were others here with you in the past, living breathing ones, but always the space between you. You, nostalgic for the time before it was decided for sure which side would win. Back when winning was thought to be… One wouldn't blame you for it. Or maybe one would. The thing about winning is… Everything that was lost is stored in the cloud, those gathering thunderheads play tricks, make you think of death. Yours and theirs. How you belong to the ones who have passed over. How you try to belong to yourself, but they are always singing their siren songs, catching your ears like a whistle to the dog. Soup that soaks deep into the marrow of bones. *They* know a little broth won't save you. At least, not today.

What string tethers this…what is it…soul? Clearly, the nightbird travels on updrafts of unconscious exhales, sighs that remember what it means to—

Inexplicable places, described never, other than to say that they are familiar buildings of stairs, passages, and rooms. What happens there lingers in a body long after it has awakened, invisibly. Flying is a possibility, as is drowning, as is falling from a great height.

After falling from a great height.

After drowning.

After flying.

After meeting a lover without a face who knows the secret corners of a heart.

The crack in the sidewalk is a mirror. The bright green weed growing out of it knows what a body is afraid to remember. The horse a body is charged with taking care of is trapped in a stall on the other side of a muddy pit of snakes. There is always a choice. Kiss the snake. Free the horse. Press the wild rose into the body until it disappears. What is it made of?

Once upon a time, a body. The body knew there were things called "stars." In the dark, it gazed up at them through something called "eyes," but no matter how hard it looked it couldn't understand.

It couldn't understand.

Later. Alone. After dark has settled around the two chairs—one empty, one still occupied, cigarette in hand. Your cigarette is tucked between thumb and forefinger. Tobacco smoke, an offering, winds its way to where your ancestors sit on clouds of dark matter and spit stars. You are a creature of the urban wilderness, an amalgam of a shining presence, the puma moving silently after prey in the moonlight. You are nothing more than a chunk of wood hacked out of a tree trunk that sits and waits to rejoin the rest of itself and does not rot but hardens to stone. Petrified. You walk in birdsong, holding memories of times you stepped outside of your mirrored prison in your cupped hands—water that sometimes flows and sometimes does not. They feed your footsteps as you track the progression of moons and suns and seasons, sparks on the horizons of the past. Ghosts and real-life boogeymen lurk around the edges of your vision. Angels.

Sometimes you try to rouse yourself from a nightmare to find that you were already awake, gasping to draw breath. It hurts. Sleep. A demon sits heavy on your chest and sings the sweetest lullabies.

You wait for morning.

MR. FIREMAN, WON'T YOU HELP ME GET HOME?

Deanne Stillman

My mother always told me that if I ever got lost, I should tell a policeman. Or if a fire station is nearby, I should go in. They'll take you home, she always told me, especially if your phone number is in your pocket, where I put it, and you should never take it out.

I know I don't look lost. As a matter of fact, people are always asking me for directions. Even in cities or places out in the middle of nowhere where I don't live and I'm walking around for the first time, someone will always stop me and ask where a certain street or store is. Maybe it's because I'm a Taurus. You know, grounded. An earth sign. I even have Taurus rising. So I'm twice as grounded, they tell me, and I guess it shows.

Do I belong everywhere? Well, some places don't ring my chimes so I don't think so. But if I went to the upper peninsula of Michigan in winter time—a season I do not like and I'm not crazy about forests, although maybe I would meet wolves—I bet someone would cross my trail and ask me which way to Ypsilanti or the Circle K.

But none of this is the main event as they say. Awhile ago, I had a dream that I was a leaf. I was being blown around all over the place. I had become detached from my tree and there I went. I felt so alone and bereft and I just didn't know what to do. As a leaf, I could not explain my predicament, and who would believe me anyway? I floated this way and that, seeking my tree, but it was not to be found.

Time passed and I found a firehouse and I went in and I said to the fireman, *I am a leaf without a tree.* And the fireman said, *Do you have a home?*

I guess you can call me daughter, I said, and he said, *Daughter, do you know where you live?* I explained how I used to live in a tree but somehow I had become separated and now I knew not how to find it. *My mother always said if you ever get in big trouble, turn yourself into the nearest fire station and they will help you.*

Can you give me some clues? the fireman asked. *Perhaps I can take you to it.*

That's the thing, I told him. *It was just a tree, in the middle of nowhere and everywhere. I am no longer part of it and I have no attachment, you see.*

Daughter, he said, *you seem like you could use a blanket.* He retrieved one and placed it over my knees. *Would you like some tea?*

Oh, that would be grand, I replied. "Grand" was a word my mother used and I liked having the opportunity to repeat it. After awhile, he returned with a mug of tea and I sipped it and that felt right.

Daughter, is there anything that you can remember about the tree? Perhaps that can help us find it.

It defies description, I said. *I am a leaf without a tree and that's all I know. Wait, I take that back. You could say that the tree has been felled by time in a land far away and thus did my life as an unattached leaf begin.*

Daughter, the fireman said, *who died?*

My mother, I said.

I am so sorry, he said. *What else should I know?*

We had a picnic on a roof, I explained. It was on top of the home where she was living and dying. I had stopped on the way, and picked up a hotdog from Nathan's—her favorite thing in the whole world. I slathered it with ketchup, just how she liked it and I bought clams for me. I walked down Coney Island Avenue to her home, holding the package close, making sure things were just so. Oh, she was thrilled. She teared up and then I said, Let's go to the patio for a picnic. It's a glorious day! Up on the roof, I laid out place settings and we unwrapped our meals, and ate heartily. Some swells were coming in and the sea breeze was a delight.

But it was the wrong ocean. My mom was a California girl at heart and she missed all of the kooky people with striped hair in psychedelic clothes on the boardwalk. She loved the guy with the dreadlocks on roller skates, the one who played Hendrix all day long. Is he still there? she asked. What about the girl who made that lovely necklace? She was referring to the one I was wearing, which she had asked the girl to put together just for me. The beads were sky blue and emerald green—my favorite colors. Everyone always asks me about the necklace, I said. It was a beauty. Oh, she's still there, Mom, I said. I love this necklace.

A little while later we went down to the boardwalk. My mom was in her wheelchair and I wrapped her cashmere scarf—the navy blue one from Brooks Brothers—around her shoulders and loosely around her neck. She was a connoisseur of fine things and she ran her fingers up and down it as I pushed her along the planks. It fluttered in the wind and she turned toward the sun. She loved getting a tan and I fully expected her to ask me when we returned to her room if she got any color. She used to mix up a bottle of baby oil and iodine whenever we went swimming and that always did the trick. The sun was not strong enough for tanning that day, and on the way back to her room, she started singing, "California here I come…" This was sort of a joke, because she had a terrible voice, and we both kind of laughed, and we both kind of cried, for we knew she would not be able to return.

Back in her room, the nurses lifted her out of her chair and helped her into bed. Then they left for the evening and I turned on the old movie channel and we watched Fred and Ginger dance and dance. And then she slept and I walked to the subway, passing the Wonder Wheel—the famous ride that promised new thrills with every turn. The ride was no longer in service; the cups that you could sit on while the Ferris wheel went round and round were still and you could not board them. The ride was just a memory of another time but on the sign flashed—Wonder Wheel Wonder Wheel—and you could always get a hotdog at Nathan's.

Come with me, the fireman said, extending his hand. *Come with me*. I took his hand and we left the station, and the next thing I know, we are boarding the Ferris wheel on the pier and we're sitting in a cup and then the wheel starts turning and he points to the Big Dipper as we circle higher and I reach for it and then down we go and then around and around again. "Welcome home, daughter," he says. "Welcome home."

PART TWO

INTERVENTIONS

A COLD SPOT

Rebecca Kuder

1976

It's October, and I'm sitting by myself on the school bus, heading to a new school, new because I've only been going here a little more than a month. Trees span the back driveway—to the right of the school and the left, covering the playground, and just…trees everywhere. A schoolyard full of trees. The trees are quiet this morning—and all the time—but alive. Sleeping statues, their leaves now turning lemon-lime. Soon I will turn ten.

On the bus while it's still moving, James comes over, says, "Bryce wants to know will you go with him."

"No," I say, and he walks away. On the bus, when I'm trapped on the bus, this happens every day.

I know what *go with* means, and I don't want to go with Bryce or anyone. I'm in fifth grade.

I'm not used to riding the bus. To get to my old school, I biked through town and past the college amphitheater where I played a townschild in *The Music Man* for the bicentennial. In the play, I cartwheeled across the stage. To get to my old school, it was bike tires bumping on the curvy path through the grassy field that was once a golf course. There were even golf tournaments, so I have heard. I've seen people hit golf balls there, and everyone still calls it the golf course, but all I see now is the overgrown field that kids bike through to get to school, or older kids do other stuff. I don't really know what older kids do there, just—I've heard about it. An expanse of green. Green and green and green. And that path is also how we walk from my old school to the college gym, to jump on the huge trampoline, or to dive into the swimming pool, in winter, my damp hair freezing into sticks on the walk back to school. And that path is how we walk to the college science lab, where we dissect dead frogs. We do a lot of things at my old school. We go to the college for science and gym even though we're just kids. We go to *college* at my old school. We have freedom. Free is even part of the name, the Antioch Free School.

Now the sleeping trees are quiet but the bus is loud and weird and here is James always with the asking. Every day James asks for Bryce because maybe Bryce is shy, or because James knows me from when we were at the free school, the best school, better than this school, Mills Lawn, where the bus is taking me now.

With everyone else, I get off the bus, pass the chalked four-square grid on the pavement, and go inside where people are loud and too many and even though I have a couple friends here from my free school, here is not what I'm used to. We sit at desks. We have a different type of cubby, everything is different. It's more uptight and clean-ish here. I am in Mr. Bright's homeroom. Each kid has a cubby. Somehow I get the job of Cubby Control, which is to be a squealer when kids cram too much stuff in their cubbies, make a mess. I am to put stickers on cubbies, and I am free to make any type of face on the stickers, smileys when the cubby is under control. Weird eyes and goofy-toothed mouths or whatever I want when it needs work. The face making is fun because I can draw all different stuff, and I do. I like and also don't like being on Cubby Control, because the control part makes people like and also not like me.

Here you get teased if you're from the free school, what that kid Marvin calls a sorry school. *Antioch's a sorry school, Antioch's a sorry school*, that kid Marvin sings at me, *stings at me*, whenever he sees me, all the time.

On the front sidewalk at Mills Lawn, one time I used my first ever lip gloss and then dropped it on the cement, and I freaked because I loved that stuff even though it made my tongue and teeth feel weird and waxy and I also freaked because the glass tube broke into pieces and the sticky gloss oozed into the pores of the cement and I didn't know what to do, how to clean it, and somehow—at that exact moment—the janitor came out and yelled at me. *Stupid girl with your stupid lip gloss,* he might as well have said.

At Mills Lawn you get in worse trouble than being yelled at sometimes. Sometimes you get *treed,* like a kid who had done something I don't know what, but during recess that kid had to sit, no freedom, could only sit at the foot of a sleeping tree statue on the school side. He was not allowed to cross the driveway with everyone else, not allowed to play.

The Free School

Why did I leave the best school in the world? I had to switch to Mills Lawn because Mills Lawn didn't cost anything, at least not money. The Antioch School was called a free school but it wasn't free to go there, not free at all.

The year before, my two earliest friends from the free school switched to Mills Lawn. We didn't have that much money, but my mom wanted one more year for me at the free school, a year in the Older Group, called the OG. A year on my own, beyond the sway of my friends who sometimes bossed me. Maybe Mom thought it would help me be more independent. Like Independence Day for our bicentennial, like *The Music Man* but without the seventy-six trombones. My year in the OG was hard—a fourth grader, youngest of the group, because the OG was fourth, fifth, sixth graders, and even older, all tossed in together.

The OG occurred in a big classroom with a loft that darkened most of the sky, so the room was like a cave and somewhat treacherous, full of older kids, who were okay sometimes, but sometimes they said older kid stuff and acted scary. Sitting, standing, splayed out, lying down wherever they wanted for reading. On couches, stools, the floor, the bookshelf. Wherever. Everywhere! There was no Cubby Control in the OG at the free school.

The OG teacher and general boss of the school was Will.

Someone—a student in the OG—scrawled across the wall: *Will Will Kill*. Maybe because in OG we sang the *Ann Boleyn with her head tucked underneath her arm* song, and the *Sad when that great ship went down* song, the *husbands and wives, little children lost their lives* song. Songs of murder and disaster. The school had a shed where the oldest OG kids opened a gambling casino. Our class pet was a boa constrictor named King. There was a dead baby shark in a bucket!

I peddled to school on the bumpy path, and although we sang murder and disaster and the cave of the OG had its shadows and barbs, I had no idea how badly 1976 was about to dislocate everything. There should have been a yellow sign in the golf course to warn me as I rode away from that free school: *More Barbs Ahead*.

My birthday fell two weeks after the deadline for fifth grade. Mom convinced the Mills Lawn principal to let me into fifth anyway, because at the free school it hadn't mattered that I was born two weeks late. She convinced him, because really I was almost old enough, and so that I could be with my earliest friends, my littermates ever since our parents had lived by each other at the college when we were tiny. Being in the fifth grade with those other puppies was helpful, though maybe it didn't matter that much because at Mills Lawn, fourth and fifth were together anyway in the part of the school called Centaurus. Why Centaurus? No one ever explained.

1976

There are fifty states. You probably know that. I might have known that at the free school, but never had to name them all, never had to *do* anything about all those states. At the free school, we learned a lot but we didn't really notice we were learning. We just did stuff and made stuff and figured stuff out. In fifth grade at Mills Lawn, everyone knows the fifty states, everyone has already memorized them, even capitals probably. The kids carry facts around in their pockets like it's no big whoop, and I am a lost baby because of everything I don't know. But I am in the purple book for math, which is advanced. Mr. Bright, the math teacher, likes me. I don't know why he likes me. Maybe because I'm in the purple book. Maybe also because I'm in his homeroom. Or maybe just because I'm new, and he's a kind teacher, even though something about him also reminds me of a cranky owl.

2017

Decades later—when I am an adult, and a parent—Mom will tell me that Will of the OG was very sorry to see me go. When I am forty-five and my own kid attends that free school, Will will have retired but will still teach math, part-time. By then, the OG will be much tamer. Will will not kill at all. Instead he will be my kid's teacher, and will confirm what Mom said, about my childhood departure from freedom, that he was sorry to see me go. He will be old, by then, and won't speak much, but as a part-time math teacher, what he scribbles on the chalkboard— something about how he shows kids the math—will make perfect sense to my kid, will unlock secret doors of understanding in her brain. She will learn well from Will. She will do some math work on a paper, and he will look at the paper and hand it back to her, and mumble, "Show this to your mom." After school she will show it to me, her advanced and beautiful math work, offer it up in the same way I will receive it, like a gold nugget.

1976

At the Mills Lawn tornado drill, we hide in a cramped closet in the center of the library, in the center of the school. Mr. Bright funnels all the kids from homeroom into the closet, counts to make sure we're all here. This school is a weird building, with this dark closet hidden in the middle of everything. The library closet is even more cave-like than the OG. We practice hiding from tornadoes because in 1974, a tornado tore through Xenia, which is nine miles from our town. That day, the tornado day, in our town, we watched green smudge the sky, and hail the size of baseballs, and I hid in our bathtub under a thick blanket because we didn't have a basement. Even though this sheltering in the library closet now is just a drill, I'm scared, thinking *tornado*. It's cramped in the back of the closet, it's dark, and I need to move to the front because, though I haven't told anyone, during summer, Mom's boyfriend touched me between my legs, and I didn't like it—maybe that's why I feel so terrible being trapped like this. It's a new word I learn in this closet, *claustrophobia*.

Another day, recess. On the way outside, Bryce stops me, says stuff, teases me—as always—about my chin, the dimple. With his thumb, he pinches at the dimple, over and over like always, even though I hate when he does that; he keeps doing it, so I slap him. Then he gets extra mad, and whams his hands against my ears. (This is called having your ears boxed, which I only learn after that moment, and I don't know why *boxed* unless it's something boxers do, or it means like drawing a box around someone's head, but all I know when it *actually* happens is that it hurts really bad.) Then he grabs a stick and breaks it over my head. A stick! It hurts, but I'm not bleeding.

We both get in trouble. We both have to go to the office to write down our accounts of what happened. *Who started it?* We both get treed. Even James has to write what happened because he saw it all, as it happened. He was a witness. James is my friend but he's also Bryce's friend. He seems to be on Bryce's side more than mine. I don't know and I will never know if our accounts match, if what they write is true. I just write what happened. I explain it somehow. I know I shouldn't slap someone, but Bryce pinched my chin, made fun of my dimple, and he wouldn't stop, and I don't care if he did it because he liked me, that's no excuse. And all that ear boxing and break- ing a stick over my head, why? I bet Bryce got in even more trouble, maybe even at home, because *you shouldn't hit a girl.* I got in trouble maybe because even more than a slap, my nails were too long, so when I slapped him, I scratched his cheek. Accident! Accidental! Because he was teasing me and I reacted. Who started it? Whose fault, really?

In 1976, Mom has no idea that her boyfriend molested me. Because when he touched me, he said *don't tell anyone*, and I don't tell anyone, I simply hate him more.

Which is why, one night when that boyfriend is leaving our house, I stand at the door while they are talking, while Mom is saying one of the goodbyes that takes five hours, where the adults keep blabbing forever.

"Bye," I say, trying to make it happen.

He doesn't go. Blah blah blah.

"Bye," I say. No one is doing anything, just talking.

Maybe Mom thinks my saying *Bye* over and over is rude, and she's right, it is. Being rude doesn't feel good, actually everything about it feels really bad. But I hate him and always, I just want him to leave my house.

Some day, years later, I will tell Mom what he did.

Being treed is a weird punishment (or a curious invention?). Everyone walks out to recess, but those who are treed (like me and Bryce) have to sit by an assigned tree. Whoever is not treed (which is almost everyone) can cross the driveway to run around and play. On the other side of the driveway, over there, is the tall slide, and the tetherball, and a field, and lots more trees, especially one particularly huge tree with roots emerging from the earth. Between those roots, sometimes I gather acorns and stuff, make up games to play, and let the roots of the tree become a natural doll house. I weave birds' nests, using maple twirlers as birds. Those twirler birds lay eggs that are actually pebbles. When I am treed, I sit by my tree, wishing I could cross the driveway and play. All I am allowed to do is sit. Public humiliation. Bryce has to do the same thing at another tree, a couple of trees away from me. I can partway see him.

From across the driveway, the tree with the dollhouse at its feet says, "Hey."

I don't answer right away.

"I'm talking to you," the tree says.

The tree leans toward me slightly, very slightly, so the kids playing tetherball or sliding or running around the field don't notice. Still I don't say anything.

The tree where I sit exhales. Its bark slackens, gets a little looser, softer. There has always been a cold spot at the base of my spine, a frozen part of me. I feel that cold spot softening, melting.

My tree says, "You don't have to speak. You don't have to explain anything. We saw it all. You don't have to convince us. Just lean back. We can hold you." At the chilly base of my spine, my tree eases itself toward me. My frozen part melts a little more.

"He shouldn't have broken a piece off you," I tell the dollhouse tree.

"Nobody should break anything off anyone. But I'm okay. Those pieces fall off sometimes. He found that stick on the ground. Just something left over. A spare part. I didn't need it anymore. He didn't break me. He couldn't, even if he tried. I go way, way down. Someday you will too."

My tree says, "You can lean back on me. Lean back."

The teacher blows the whistle, time to go back inside. Slowly I rise, refreshed and ready for math, the purple book, and walk toward school, not even looking at the tree where Bryce sits. Who cares? There's calm inside my body. My ears don't sting from the echo of being boxed anymore. But my feet tingle, bounce lightly as I step, and also pull down. I feel gravity, all in balance, and when my steps land, a soft magnet is waiting for them, solid ground, supporting me, like I don't have to worry anymore about being teased, or being scared, or naming all the states or feeling lost on the bus or in the world, or feeling small. Or being invisible, or being mute.

Because now, I get to say what I want, what I don't want. Now I get to choose how and whether you touch me.

Look around! See all those trees?

OF THREE MINDS:
A FREUDIAN FAIRY TALE

Laura Cline

Right in the middle of a perfectly average street, there is an even more average house. The vinyl siding is beige, it's missing a couple of roof tiles, and the grass in the front is long dead. The weeds are not too overgrown and the gate out front is made of chain link and has to be opened by hand. The street is a busy one for a small town, and the sidewalk runs only along one side. In the morning, joggers come by, young and old, in brightly colored lycra, wearing backpacks and earbuds. Bikers zip by, chatting loudly to one another about the incline of the road. And by late afternoon, there are bedraggled-looking men, dragging their bags of belongings and their dusty, cheap sleeping bags up to the woods for the night. The sounds of the road drift in through the big picture window in the living room of the house, along with dust from the yard and the sun's thick morning rays.

On the splintery telephone poles along the street, flyers blow in the wind each time a car passes. They are printed in Sharpie on computer printer paper and stuck to each pole with duct tape. They say:

WANTED

A real adult to help a couple of crazy bitches with every-day tasks. For example: motivating them to get out of bed after snoozing the alarm five to six times, doing the laundry before they run out of underwear and have to buy more at Target, picking up that one tiny scrap of trash that has been on the floor for a week and which everyone keeps tripping on, figuring out what that smell coming from the kitchen sink could be, planning how to eat all the freezer-burned food before the drawer gets so full the door won't shut and it just beeps and beeps, reminding them that thinking about stuff doesn't pay any bills, and generally keeping their you-know-what together.

If this sounds like the job for you, call (XXX)-XXX-XXXX. Pay is negotiable.

On the morning of the adulting interviews, the two residents of the house struggle to get themselves up on time. The first (let's call her The Rebel) is hungover, and her mascara is smeared under her eyes and across her white pillowcase. She wakes up, throws open the drapes, and gulps down three shots of espresso and three slices of leftover cold pizza. She plops down on the sofa in her sweatpants and stained T-shirt and turns on Netflix. She's about to start binge-watching a reality dating show, but she hears footsteps.

"Turn that off right now. We have a full day!" This is the second resident (we can call her The Perfectionist). She thinks that she has made a spreadsheet with information about each of the planned interviews that day, but she can't find it to pull it up. She is already dressed, but nothing she is wearing fits quite right. Her pants are one inch too long and her left shoe is a size too big. She has taken a shower, but the product in her hair didn't really work, so it is already frizzy. For breakfast, she takes a handful of almonds and writes "four almonds" in her food notebook.

They peer together out the front window to see the first interviewee pull up in a sensible, not old and not new Toyota Corolla at 9:23 a.m., seven minutes before her scheduled interview. She gets out of the car, and they scan her up and down. Her hair is brownish, blondish, reddish, she isn't fat or thin, and her clothes are plain: a black T-shirt, jeans, and black Converse. No trash falls out of her car when she gets out, and she remembers to walk back to shut the gate at the end of the drive.

She comes up the front walkway, looks down at her phone to make sure she isn't too early and rings the broken doorbell. There is no sound, but the door swings open and both The Rebel and The Perfectionist stand there, right inside the door. Something about the scene is a little uncanny. They are all exactly the same height and they all say "Hello" at the same time, with the exact same intonation. They look down at their shoes. They brush a piece of hair back beyond their left ears.

They sit in the living room.

The Rebel: So, how long have you been adulting?

The Candidate: Um, well, I'm thirty-nine years old, so since I was, like, twenty-seven? I mean, I don't think anyone can really adult when they are eighteen, or twenty-one, or twenty-five.

The Perfectionist: So, like, what did you do at twenty-seven that made the switch?

The Candidate: I got married, I guess? Well, engaged. I got a couple of dogs and I kept them alive. Finished grad school. Got a job. Stopped putting everything on credit cards.

The Rebel: Oh! Good one. If you get this job, one of the requirements will be holding my credit cards for me. Like, I can't stop charging all the things. I had to use my whole tax return last year to pay them off, and then I just charged 'em right up again. Like, who says jumpsuits aren't necessities? (*She laughs, but no one else does, so she looks down at her lap.*)

The Perfectionist: (*Raises hand high in the air.*) Hello, me. I've told you a million times, YOU NEED A BUDGET. You need to cut up all your credit cards except for one, and that one you need to freeze in a block of ice at the back of the freezer for emergencies. You should only buy necessities. Make a budget for groceries and use coupons. Turn off all the lights to save on electricity. Call all of your credit card companies and service providers to negotiate lower rates. Declutter the whole house. Become a minimalist by applying the Konmari method. Create a capsule wardrobe. Start making your own gifts. Focus on spending money only on experiences. You know, I read…

The Rebel: UGGGGGGGGGGH, would you shut the freak up? *(She plays with her phone for a minute.)* I just bought, like, six things on Amazon.

The Perfectionist: You see what I mean? How can I possibly take care of this *(gestures toward The Rebel)* by myself?

The Candidate: Yeah, I mean, I guess I could help you put together some kind of easy budget and clean out your closet or something?

The Rebel: Okay, well, while you are at it, could you get the stick out of this chick's ass? I mean, get her a valium or something. I don't need her to take care of me. I'm a grown woman. Stop trying to control me!

The Rebel hands the candidate a printed sheet of paper to review.

THE REBEL

Height: Crazy short

Weight: Morbidly obese although she doesn't like that term, but seriously, BMI 40.6, doctors-always-suggesting-HCG-injections-fat. Rebels by eating more food.

Employment: Scrolling through Facebook at her desk. Leaving early to go thrift shopping. Making big piles of paper everywhere. Swearing that she will go through them later, but inevitably just throwing them away after a requisite period of time. Gossiping and complaining.

Favorite foods: McDonald's Oreo McFlurries. Whole boxes of Kraft macaroni 'n' cheese made with extra butter. Sad bowls of Goldfish crackers, mixed with chocolate chips and eaten five minutes before bed.

Ailments: Sore knees, general sloth, migraines, fatigue, bitchiness, caffeine addiction, fungal infections, radical hormonal shifts.

Hobbies: Marijuana, alcohol, napping, whining, buying things online, binge eating, watching so-bad-it-is-barely-watchable reality TV.

Goals: Finding a way to make money while doing nothing, and also without having to work too hard to be able to do it.

Next, The Perfectionist hands over hers, printed on a lilac paper with an embossed stamp on top:

THE PERFECTIONIST

Height: I think it is just right.

Weight: Ideal thanks to Weight Watchers!

Job: Bossing people around, being perpetually right. Knowing what is best for everyone in every situation. Being certain that her way is the only way. Completing tasks in a timely manner. Getting things done the right way.

Favorite food: Salad.

Ailments: Random spells of hysterical crying, severe obsessive-compulsive disorder, tension headaches, TMJ, stress diarrhea, yo-yo dieting.

Hobbies: Organizing, writing to-do lists, self-flagellation, obsessing, googling illnesses, self-diagnosing, very hot yoga.

Goals: To do everything absolutely perfectly and to never ever fail or lose control.

The candidate scans the documents and nods.

The Perfectionist: Do you think you can do it? (*Her eyes are hopeful. The Rebel is picking at a callus on the bottom of one of her feet.*)

So, the bitches hire The Candidate and she becomes The Adult. She moves into their house where The Perfectionist occupies one side of the house with stark white walls and minimalist decor; the front of her stainless-steel refrigerator is covered in lists: to do, done, gratitude, gifts, groceries. The Rebel lives on the other side. She has a ratty couch and flat-screen TV and the floor is littered with empty plates and cracker crumbs, a bong, unopened mail, unpaid bills, and filthy clothes.

They walk The Adult in through the front door and show her to her room. She has to walk through a maze of discarded items—piles of books, unused pots and pans, clothes with the tags still on them, piles of lists with half the items crossed out, important documents, passports, photos. Behind all the clutter she finds the door to the tiny closet where she will sleep, an antique-looking television and a modest twin bed covered by a threadbare blanket. It isn't comfortable; there is very little space for her here.

The Perfectionist: Well, I guess we should let you unpack and settle in.

The Adult: Is there a bathroom?

The Perfectionist: Sure, it is through that door. (*She gestures toward a tiny, cabinet-sized door on the far side of the windowless room.*)

When The Perfectionist leaves, The Adult thinks about unpacking her suitcase, but with nowhere to put anything, she simply slides it underneath the bed. She opens the cabinet door, turns herself sideways to squeeze through the slit, and finds a restroom that looks like it has fallen straight out of a passenger jet, with a tiny fire-prevention-type showerhead in the center of the ceiling. She slides back out and shuts the door.

She walks into the living area and starts to get to work, figuring she can complete no other tasks until she makes the home where they live accessible. She starts with the lists, cramming them into some discarded grocery bags she finds lying on the floor. She takes each filled bag out and places it in the trash until the can is so full the top bulges open on its hinge. Suddenly, the house feels just a little less full and there is just a little more room for The Adult.

She keeps at it over the next several weeks. She cleans out all the trash in The Rebel's rooms, and she washes and puts away all the dirty clothes. Strangely, as she cleans these things out, her room gets bigger. After the first few days, a dresser appears so that she can unpack and make herself at home. A real shower with glass walls and a normal width door appears in the tiny bathroom after the first week.

One day, while she is washing the residue out of the bong in the sink, The Perfectionist comes in, startling her.

The Perfectionist: *(scoffs)* Well, there you are. I almost thought you had quit. You haven't been up to see me at all.

The Adult: Oh, I mean, I kind of thought you had it all together…I thought it was more about, you know…(*She nods in the direction of The Rebel, who is lying on the sofa and watching an actual sitcom that most people seem to find amusing.*)

The Perfectionist: Well, obviously she is the bigger problem, but that doesn't mean that there isn't anything you can do for me.

The Adult: Oh, okay. I would be happy to help with whatever it is…

The Perfectionist: I. Don't. Know. What. It. Is. Ugh. If I knew what I needed, I would just do it. Can't you see? I can do anything, and I can do it perfectly. (*The Adult glances down at The Perfectionist's unzipped fly.*) So why do I feel so empty? I tried a keto diet, eliminating gluten, eating for my astrological sign. I read four books about how to find my joy. I bought a goal-setting planner with tons of matching stickers. I set my intention and breathe deeply for four full minutes before starting my day. Every. Single. Day.

The Adult: Okay… How does that make you feel?

The Perfectionist: (*She releases one loud sob and then wipes frantically under her eyes.*) Pull yourself together!

Before The Adult can say anything else, The Perfectionist runs into her room.

Over the next few days, The Adult starts sneaking into The Perfectionist's room while she is at spin class. She crosses out items on the to-do lists, even though they would be left undone. She starts leaving treats around the house that she knows The Perfectionist won't be able to resist. The Perfectionist comes home to a slice of German chocolate cake on a placemat with the good silverware at the table, a warm bath with a lovely smelling bath bomb, or a book on her pillow with an irresistible storyline that keeps her up late reading. She smiles more. Jokes are a little funnier. She finds a few shows she likes watching on Netflix, and she sits down right next to The Rebel, lacing their fingers together as they watch. Sometimes she even skips a workout or lets the dishes sit in the sink overnight.

The Adult hopes that now that she has cleaned up the trash and removed the thick window coverings from her rooms, The Rebel will start to come around as well. She empties all of the alcohol from her mini-fridge. She scrubs the tiles in her bathroom until they shine. But still, she finds The Rebel lying on the dirty couch, scrolling through her phone with trash TV in the background.

The Adult: Hey, do you want to come outside with me, maybe take a walk around the block?

The Rebel: Ummmm, let me think about it. No. Would you like to sit with me and take a rip from this bong?

The Adult: Probably not. I haven't smoked weed since college. *(She plops down on the couch despite her reservations about sanitation.)* What is this show about?

The Rebel: A lady who pops people's pimples. I mean, she is a doctor. It's so gross. Look at all that stuff coming out of that one! Yowza! Want a Twinkie?

The Adult: Um, maybe? Are they good?

The Rebel: Yeah, they're good. Better with weed. Also, they are indestructible.

The Adult: *(opens the package and takes a bite)* I thought they would be worse. Are you sure you don't want to take a walk outside?

The Rebel: Give me a break, lady. I mean, you cleaned up down here. I'm looking at the sunshine through that horrible window. When will enough be enough?

The Adult: So you are happy then? I've done my job?

The Rebel: Freak no, I'm not happy. Look at me. *(She runs her hands up and down her body.)*

The Adult: Well, maybe if you took a walk outside and—

The Rebel: Stop trying to control me! I make my own choices. I LIKE Twinkies.

The Adult: Okay, okay. Are you crying?

The Rebel: No, it's just allergies or something. (*She chokes back a sob.*)

The Adult scoots closer. She places her hand on The Rebel's shoulder and leans into a half hug. She strokes The Rebel's hair and she slowly lowers her messy head into her lap so that she can braid and play with her hair while the two of them continue to watch TV until they eventually fall asleep.

Over the coming weeks and months, life continues in the average house on the average street. Slowly the house shifts and moves on the inside until all three occupants have the same amount of space (usually anyway). There are three bedrooms and bathrooms, each of equal size, a shared kitchen, and three cleanish sofas in the living room with just one television. The house is a little messy sometimes, but The Perfectionist is always there to remind them to pick it up. They read books and watch trashy TV, and sometimes they leave the dishes in the sink overnight. Sometimes The Rebel makes them a few champagne cocktails and they even keep the now thoroughly cleaned bong around. Every night they take a walk around the block.

THE TEA LEAF READER

Michaela Carter

My family has a tendency toward excommunication, which runs straight through my father's side in an arrow-like trajectory that feels a whole lot like a curse. Though his paternal grandmother, the tea leaf reader, can't be blamed—at least not directly—for the leaving on my father's maternal side. The arrow of absence that would be her legacy sent her beautiful motherless son (my grandfather) into the arms of a beautiful fatherless woman (my grandmother) who gave birth to three children, my father and two aunts. No family members since have abandoned their families, but they have excommunicated one another. For instance, my grandmother excommunicated my father for a good five years before she started talking to him again. Now my youngest aunt, Lynda, isn't talking to my older aunt, or to my father or to me or my children—or to my grandfather's last wife, who she kept from him at the end of his life to the very best of her means.

"My mother was mean," my grandfather said. "She threw me against a wall when I was a baby. I still have the scar on my head," he told me on his ninetieth birthday, at a party his fiancé hadn't been invited to, because Lynda, who was paying for the party, hadn't wanted her there. I sat beside him on a sofa, and he held my hand in his large, strong hand.

"*Mean*," he repeated, wide-eyed and shivering a little, as if he were still afraid of her. "She came from England," he said, and I could feel the cold dark damp of the place where my great-grandmother had been born. "I was just a baby. What sort of a mother could do that?"

Only a monster.

Nine and a half years later, at my grandfather's celebration of life, which Lynda hadn't come to because she'd excommunicated us all, my older aunt corroborated the story. "She was a witch! She read tea leaves," she said, and being a born-again Christian, she meant that she was evil. I'd already heard about the tea leaves years ago from Lynda, who thought it had made her grandmother interesting.

My grandfather's father, on the other hand, was by all accounts a sweet man. My father had adored him. When he'd take the train from Danville, Illinois, to Phoenix, Arizona, to visit his grandkids, he'd stay for a month at a time and tell them stories of bars and guns and women. His name was Vincent, and my father is named for him.

When I asked my father what my great-grandmother's name was, he shrugged and told me he had no idea, but that one day she had packed up and left, moved across town, had a whole new family and apparently never even tried to get in touch with the three children she'd left. This was unforgivable. For this sin alone, she was written out of the story of my family.

I know so little about her. This is what I know:

Fact 1: She was British.

Fact 2: She was mean.

Fact 3: She was selfish.

But she also read tea leaves, which made her a mystical monster.

I think of my nameless great-grandmother, a ghost among ghosts, when I drink my hibiscus tea and watch the leaves settle at the bottom of the cup. I see an owl facing me, or else a falcon in profile. Either way I see a predator. Something a woman cannot be. Forever the prey, meek and tasty, the ingénue; for those queens with their desires are always evil. To desire something and to pursue it makes a woman subject to suspicion and to erasure.

Monster, tea leaf reader, she lives in my blood. She is part of me. This forgotten woman who dared to desire a life she could choose—a different life—this woman who made the leap, who

left her husband and children, sings a song I can hear if I am
quiet and still, if I listen.

It was them or me, them or me.
I was young. I'd chosen badly.
He was kind to them, but not to me.
I was worth less to him than his donkey.

The tea leaves told another story.
Make a clean break, they told me.
Two parallel lines, two lives, you see?
It could be them and me, them and me.

Lights come up on a stage filled with fog. We hear a woman's
voice.

Nameless Matriarch
We are ghosts to each other, ghosts among ghosts.

Slowly the fog clears. The Author, a woman in her fifties, stands stage
right. Nameless Matriarch, a giant moth transfixed by the light, white and
otherworldly, stands stage left. The Author looks at the audience, though
she speaks to Nameless Matriarch.

Author
Your son Colby—the one you threw against the wall—
died last week. I thought you should know.

Nameless Matriarch
Perhaps he is here, where I am.

Author
Do you want to know him? Did you ever wonder what
happened to him, to all of your children?

Nameless Matriarch takes a few steps forward. A spotlight follows her.
She wipes her neck. She is dripping sweat, wretched from heat and thirst.
She squints into the spotlight, then shades her eyes with her hand so she

can see the audience. She looks from one person to the next, speaking to individuals.

Nameless Matriarch

I knew you would judge me, which is why I hid from my actions for so many years.

A clean break the leaves had said so clearly. I believed in the leaves. I understood their syntax. I left my children. All three of them, it is true! A father? A father can leave. But a mother who leaves is a monster. What will you have me do? Into what hole will you throw me, against what wall as you line up with stones in your hands?

Nameless Matriarch kneels on the floor and lowers her head. After a moment she looks up, looks the audience in the eyes, piercingly.

Nameless Matriarch

Are none of you without sin?

She stands, brushes off her skirt.

I'll tell you the truth, then. The beatings were the least of it. I couldn't breathe in that shack, all of the children so needy, pulling at my skirt, pleading, *Mummy, Mummy.* Three children right in a row.

If there had been more air, perhaps I'd not have snapped like that. All winter the snow had come down. Their father and I fought often. I was no pushover. I gave him what for when he went straight to the bars after his three-day stints building the railroad. The work was exhausting, but his family was more exhausting. He drank away the money that might have bought us food, and then he blamed me for not being able to feed him and the children.

Roy, Colby, Lana. You never forget the children you left. They haunt you. What they might look like as the years spin by, what their lives might have become.

Lana and Roy never came to see me, but after the war Colby found me. He was a pilot. So handsome. He was getting married but he had something to ask me first. He didn't ask why I left. He knew why I left, saw me in my yellow dress with the good fabric and fit and he knew. The man I married took pride in my well-being.

When Colby asked me why I never came to see them, how could I explain what I had seen that day in the tea cup—the leaves in two parallel lines—meaning peace and happiness and long life—and how the two didn't touch? *Couldn't* touch? How the two lines could only exist in peace if they didn't cross. I'd seen it so clearly. Two very distinct trajectories, two paths, arrow-straight. I had to jump tracks.

Where was your mother-love? He wanted to know. I told him that mother-love made me leave, that I knew his father would love them better in my absence.

Nameless Matriarch sits at a small table set with a tea service and two china cups. The Author sits across from her. Nameless Matriarch spoons tea leaves into each of their cups and pours hot water over them. They regard each other through the steam.

Nameless Matriarch
Ceylon black. From England, my mother used to send it to me. True British tea. The kind civilized people drink. Not those rough types that don't know their ass from their elbow.

They pick up their cups, blow on the hot water to cool it.

Nameless Matriarch
Hold your question in your mind. Do you have it?

Author
I do.

They drink the hot tea slowly.

Nameless Matriarch
Leave a little water in the bottom for the spirits.

With her left hand, Nameless Matriarch swirls the tea three times from left to right. She turns the cup over on the saucer. She leaves it that way for a minute and then rotates it three times and turns it right side up. They peer into the cup. In unison, they raise their heads and look at each other. Nameless Matriarch's antennae twitch.

Nameless Matriarch
Doris. My name is Doris Moss Slightam.

The light on the table fades. The Author walks to center stage. A spotlight shines on her. There is a sepia filter on the light and soon ripples of light, as one might see at the bottom of a creek, move across her. She looks as if she were made of water. She stands with her legs hips-width apart. Grounded. She is barefoot. Her arms are stretched out wide at her sides. She lifts her face to the upper balcony of the theater. The light shines brightest on her chest, where her heart is, and then the brightness swells, growing large enough to include Doris inside its waters which stretch to the edges of the stage and beyond them, rippling across the curtains and the theater, over the audience itself; all are washed in the water-light which begins to swirl.

Doris rises from her chair, walks to the Author and takes her hand. They bow. Strangely, the audience remains quiet. They do not believe it's the end.

Doris exits. The swirling light slows and stills. The stage goes dark, save for a sepia spotlight on the Author. Over her face and body shadows shaped like tea leaves settle.

Lights out.

GRIEF BECOMES THE THING THAT HOLDS US

Mariel Berger

When my mom dances, I love her the most. She bends down with her hands on her knees, butt sticking out, and does a little twist, her head moving from side to side. She grins coyly with her eyes squinting, like she knows exactly how cute she is. Her favorite song, "Gloria," is playing, as she sways to the beat in her long red dress, which matches the fiery highlights streaked along her short dark hair. Her knees have hurt her for years but somehow, for the span of the dance, she bends them freely. My mom dances by herself, none of the men she tried to love are there, but I imagine she's there dancing with her younger selves too, the child with the dark bold eyes, the poet with the long black hair. They're all dancing together, laughing. My mom, the older one, looks over her shoulder and winks at me.

Sometimes I play this scene of her dancing and singing on repeat, as if I play it enough, all the other moments will be squeezed out.

❧

I don't remember much about my old homes. There is the door from my fourth or fifth house, the one in South Jersey, before the other house, before the other house. I don't remember any other detail, not even the color of my room's walls. But that door I can see so clearly. It's white with horizontal slits. I knew they were behind it because they were nowhere else. I had silently and secretly checked all the other rooms. I opened that laundry room door and my life completely changed, or my life had already imploded but this was me fully seeing it.

I remember opening it, screaming, and then running upstairs to my sister, my sister who wouldn't believe me, not until my screaming and sobbing spoke the truth for me. My mom and her lover ran upstairs to console us, but by then the household had completely crumbled and you don't trust the person who set the bomb to hold you in your shaking.

Nathan doesn't understand a broken home the way I do, like a boulder crashed down onto me, onto my family. He still has his childhood home to return to, and in it, both of his parents, still together.

❧

I have a lot of experience throwing up, Mom mentions casually as she holds back my wavy brown short hair while my face hovers over the toilet. I am thirty-six. I had just fled Thanksgiving dinner due to my severe and chronic acid reflux, and she had followed, sensing I needed her. She strokes my back: *Oh, you poor thing, just let it out. Poor thing.* My hands grip the cold tiles on the floor as my stomach erupts.

As the food falls, as my throat is on fire, I hear another moan from far away, from the past—a sound buried deep within my belly under layers and layers of food. This is the burning in my gut, my sister's memory of my mother's bulimic past, recently revealed to me:

Dinner is almost over. I am fourteen. My sister, and now stepdad, Jim, and I are at the kitchen table eating spaghetti. Mom runs to the bathroom, and then the sound as she vomits, the sound as the food goes the wrong way. All that nourishment leaving. The sound of the flush. She coughs and clears her throat. I eat in the other room not hearing anything but the fork scraping, my pasta slurping into my mouth. I chew the food that has absorbed the sound of the retching. I swallow the memory into my belly.

❧

I have three pictures of my mom taken seconds apart. The first two photos she's smiling at the camera. In the third, she recoils—her head down, eyes big, face seized. She remains frozen in the time when she was a teenager and beaten by her father.

I was physically abused for five years, she says. *I couldn't defend myself, but I never backed down, which made him hit more, mostly with fists to my head and face. There often was blood, swelling, then scars.*

She tells her story not to release it, but to hold it tighter. She squeezes her dark eyes, purses her lips.

Once when I was sixteen, my father hit me over the head with my guitar, breaking it.

The creases in her face grow tighter as she tells me.

It was my only instrument, the only thing that brought me peace. And he used it as a weapon.

I hear the cracking of the guitar, the warped pitches of the strings as it hits her head.

She relives it every day. Anytime someone near her makes a sudden movement, even just to cough, she flinches as if she's being attacked.

My grandpa left World War II only to come home and continue the battle on my teenage mother. He buried tiny mines inside her body that, once stepped upon, cause her to explode in fear and anger. Her face still clenches from being struck, her lips grip together tightly, unable to relax enough to let a meal find its way through. My mom's eating disorder has shifted over the years from bulimia to severe anorexia. She is so frail and shrunken, I worry that she'll shatter when I hug her. Bones stick out of her face, her jaw protrudes. Sometimes I wonder if there's anything under her skin.

I want her to heal. I want her to eat. I want to go to that moment and shield her from my grandpa, move him away, stop him from hitting her. *Don't do this,* I'd plead. *The war has taken your humanity from you, but don't hit your daughter. Please. Give me something else to remember you by. I want to remember you by the way that you loved baseball and the beach, and the times you would take my sister and me out for ice cream and sing opera in the car. I want to remember your shiny green glasses that reflected the sun pouring through your kitchen. I want to remember your huge, heavy flashlight with the round button, the one I was using when I discovered that Santa Claus did not exist—that it was you wrapping presents in the dark under the tree. I want to remember the way that you would laugh so loud and full, and send me a Valentine's Day card every year. I want to remember how we shared the same birthday, how rare that was, how lucky I was to share it. Please, put the guitar down so I can love you more freely in my memories.*

Put the guitar down so I can love Nathan more easily.

❧

My comfort food is mac 'n' cheese, the kind from the box with the orange powdered cheese and mushy, cylindrical noodles. I first had it when I was with a babysitter, feeling scared to be without my parents, and I remember the softness of the macaroni felt like a pillow, the squishy, cheesy noodles made me feel warm and safe.

Nathan's lips feel like macaroni 'n' cheese.

❧

The pond in New Hampshire is frozen solid. Nathan wants to walk on it.

He smiles. *It's safe, it's safe. Don't worry.*

We had just watched the pond from high above in the cabin, as the clouds shifted to uncover the sun. The snowy surface slowly turned from gray to bright white as the light moved from one side of the pond to the other. This was the same blue-green pond that we swam in five months ago, feeling the algae tickling our feet, watching the orange fish scurrying below us, hearing the muffled laughter from the dock where other family members sat.

Come. He gently takes my hand to step onto the white pond.

He tells me there are thirteen inches of solid ice between us and the water, thirteen inches of ice, which create the separation of the summer pond and the winter pond. Just thirteen inches between the past and the present.

I step onto the pond and slowly walk above the past. My legs are shaking, my feet crunching in the uneven snow. Am I able to walk on water merely because time has passed? Merely because the temperature has dropped?

Nathan is walking faster in front of me in his bright orange hat, confident he won't fall in, confident of those thirteen inches, and I am walking slowly, looking down, dizzy. If there is a clear patch without snow, can I look through the ice and see the past? Will I see us there swimming? Can my swimming-self look up and see me? Does this pond contain all of the moments at once, layered together?

A bald eagle soars in front of us, its majestic black wings supporting a snowy white head. We hear the echoes of the loon calling from the summer below us, as we feel our feet crunching in the snow, as we see the eagle up ahead, toward which we go…toward which we go.

Losing the key began the fight. We scrambled all morning to find Nathan's car key, and then he left in a hurry to talk to his ex, giving me a hollow hug goodbye. I march myself to Prospect Park to kick the snow, to break the thin iced lake. I throw a stick onto the lake, but it doesn't even make a dent. I think about jumping on the lake until it cracks open, until I crack open, awoken by the cold. This is different than in New Hampshire—a different water, a thinner ice. I try to let it out so it isn't smothering me—the tension in my shoulders, the cramping in my stomach—Mom and Grandpa's rage.

This is a path that I usually come to walk slowly and gaze at the glistening seagulls on the sparkling lake. Sometimes some of the water is melted, and other parts are frozen with snow. The melted parts look like blue polka dots, and the frozen parts looked like islands of white fire, shimmering in the sun. Sometimes the geese suddenly fly upward in unison, from the lake into the sky, forming a V that arranges and rearranges in the clouds, their wings making a squeaky sound in the wind, their beaks honking in song.

But now, I only notice the slush and my thumping heart that feels like it is trying to tear through my rib cage, break through my skin, and fly into the air. I try to breathe and stomp until it passes, but when I come home my body is still shaking. I call Nathan.

I'm so angry.

I'm sorry you're angry.

Bria was having a hard time, he says. This was the first time the two of them had spoken in a year.

I'm not in love with her, he says. *I love you.*

My heart is racing, but I stop talking, pause, and let his words in.

I figured out where the key must be! I say, later that night. *Remember when I crouched behind that tree, in the woods in the park to pee? It must have fallen out then.*

Well go back and look for it, he says. *Just look for your yellow pee on the snow.*

Maybe it will glow in the dark? I say.

He laughs in a guttural way, like he always does at my jokes, and I can finally breathe.

The key is near the pee, we sing. *The key is near the pee.*

I'm not sure you're my life partner, Nathan says. He tells me this, like he doesn't see that I'm already standing on a beaten, cracked, wobbly floor—a house with no foundation. He can't give me something I have never even known. My house is trembling, he's wavering, and I can't hold onto him to stop from falling. Everything around me is moving—I'm bawling, dizzy, shaking—my stomach churns. The intense crying triggers my acid reflux and I run to the bathroom and throw up. Nathan strokes my hair—*Mare Bear, are you okay? Are you okay?*

I remember how recently my mom called to tell me:

I was so sick yesterday. It must have been food poisoning. I was hovered over the toilet for hours, crying for my mom.

And now I see us both, kneeling in broken prayer on the cold bathroom floor, our heads bent, our mouths open to let out a sound...

Mom and I are singing together, a song I wrote—"Hymn for Grace." I am thirty-four, this is her favorite song of mine. The smell of Mom's homemade tomato sauce from the kitchen radiates through the living room, layered with our music that also fills the air—like the sound and smell are in a duet. Mom looks into my eyes during the chorus, which is just the word *grace* repeating over and over, stretching high into the ashen clouds and then slowly descending like a sigh. Each time we sing the word, we try again to lift up...

I am nine. Mom is tucking me under my Rainbow Brite sheets and is singing the Motown song—"Goodnight Sweetheart." She strokes my hair as I sing along and try to reach the very low bass part—*do do do do do,* which makes us both laugh. We sing harmony in the verses together—the song is weaving us together, holding us both. I am singing, but also drifting into dreams, but then there is a crashing sound from far in the future...

I am twenty-two. Mom is banging the computer.

We're in her tiny apartment she's renting in South Jersey, in her bedroom. She screams at me, *You ruined it! You ruined the one thing that helps me see other people!*

The computer was her way out from loneliness; she was making friends, going on dates, and I had messed it up by downloading a virus. This is twelve years after she cheated on my dad with Jim, and after Jim had then cheated on her. So many homes destroyed, so many last names discarded.

She throws the light gray Dell monitor onto the floor and strikes the hard drive, kicking it to the ground. I can't breathe or move, but then I run from her bedroom and frantically pack my things to get out of there. She drags the computer piece by piece to the blue dumpster in front of the apartment building, and I run from the house sobbing. Afterward, a family friend helped her carry the computer back from the dumpster to the house, and fixed the virus.

She has never been violent toward me, but for that moment I couldn't help think: *She destroys the computer instead of hitting me.*

When Mom is attacking the computer, I can imagine my grandpa is also there, hitting her. He can't really see her, he's got the war in his eyes and he's running from gunfire. He's screaming, my mom is screaming, and now I enter the room. Present me. I go to younger Me who is huddled in the corner trembling, and I hold her into me. I hold her, I hold my aching belly, and I start to weep—deep painful sobs that sound like the earth's grief scraping through me, like I'm giving birth to a wretched, mangled sorrow.

My grandpa-with-the-war-in-his-eyes hears the crying, looks over, and fully sees me. He sees that his hitting hits far into the future, that it hurts me too. He sees me with my pain breaking open, stops hitting, stumbles to the ground, and howls and cries like he did when he was a boy. And Mom, now no longer being hit, stops attacking the computer. She falls to the ground, cradles her stomach, and wails and wails.

The endless salt water pours out of us and starts to fill up the apartment. There's water swirling through the room, through us. Our tears become sparkly ocean waves that burst down the walls, and the floor of the room turns into a boat that drifts on the pulsing tide. Grandpa, Mom, and I sail on the boat in the bright open air, our emerald tears rushing from our eyes into the glittering sea on which we float.

Our grief becomes the thing that holds us.

I stretch my hand on my forehead like a visor under the beaming sun, and look out into the vastness. Is this the same sea Grandpa took me to as a kid? It must be.

Grandpa! I say. *We just cried out your favorite Long Island green ocean!* Grandpa laughs, an enormous tremolo, like an operatic aria, which shakes the boat, and then Mom laughs, a high-pitched, ecstatic scream. I echo Mom in a giant roar, and this is a different kind of story that is now passing down through generations of time. The vibration of the laughter rounds and softens my belly. I am in a different kind of home now that is shaking, but I see that maybe movement can also be okay. Maybe we pretend to build houses on land that won't crumble or change, maybe we pretend to know for sure, maybe Nathan is giving me all that there ever is.

The Liquor Store Tree

Kara Hollowell

Spring

She loves to stand on the sofa while looking out the window. And I love watching her do it. I get in trouble when I put my feet on the cushions, but adults can do whatever they want. Our chunky house phone is tucked in her chin, and she's whispering into the receiver. I can hear the words from my hiding spot in the hallway. *Hurry, come, free, excited.*

Every day, four o'clock sharp, the man's truck drives by. I can hear his engine slowing down as she waves and blows a kiss. She's golden.

But then she hangs up the phone and her face goes numb and sunken. All color fades. She drags the phone with her as she walks right through me. I always regret not jumping out in front of her to intercept that kiss.

I run back to my room and close the door quietly. I pull out my book of fairytales and bury myself inside.

Momma left us to become a tree. She's the tallest one in town. She stands beside the liquor store parking lot, swaying and looking down on everyone. I don't know why she wanted to leave. But I think she's happier now.

I like to walk by after school and see her dancing in the breeze. There's a new puddle of brown water at her trunk, so I think she has enough to drink. She's so tall the telephone wires string through her leaves. She casts shade and needles down onto the black cement and buds of old cigarettes. Sometimes, if I stand around long enough, some of her soft points sprinkle down and softly prick my skin.

Dad says I shouldn't walk this way. *Nothing good comes from a street like that.* I know I should take the school bus home. But I like the walk and passing through town is the only time I can really see Momma.

Cinderella's mom is a tree too. She grants wishes and listens to Cinderella's hardships.

But Momma doesn't grant wishes and I don't remember her ever listening.

Her quiet seems lighter now. I like to go up and put my hand on her trunk. She's so rough and dark. Maybe if I cry onto her roots she'll turn back into a person. And then we'll ride off in a pumpkin carriage.

There's another difference between Cinderella's mom and mine.

Her mom died and mine's still alive.

The man in the truck did something new last night. It was long past four, but he came back again. His Ford slowed to a complete stop, and he flashed his lights three times. I heard Momma zip up those long black boots she likes to wear on weekends. I heard the door shut and the whole house went quiet.

Then the truck went away.

Summer

Granny's cookouts are the best. Me and my brothers, Alex and Baby, crawl under the picnic table and wait. Soon enough, little treasures drop down between the stained wood. Crumbs from a hamburger, half-melted chocolates from Auntie's pockets, and Dad's big, sunburned hand pinching our cheeks.

Eventually, their conversations become hushed and serious, and they forget all about us. Occasionally we're kicked or nudged by a dirty flip-flop, but it's worth it.

Finally, the grand prize is won. A tag-team effort between my brothers' distractions and my sticky fingers. I tuck the half-full red solo cup under my dress, and we run to the woods to add the treasure to our collection.

These trees look nothing like Momma. They shield us from the summer's sun and beckon us with bending limbs to march deeper into the cool path. Our secret fort is just past the pond. But you need to earn its protection. We take turns like ants, my brothers first and me in the rear, half crawling across the fallen pine that floats in the water. The log is strong but thin, so one wrong step means you're going into the dead-mosquito-coated murk.

Our precious base is a culmination of fallen treasures. We made the perimeter out of green and black bottles, Auntie's old scarves, and Granny's tablecloths made into strong walls.

Alex took a sip; baby-brother winced; I looked around, feeling guilty. Dad used to always take this juice away from Momma even though without it she withered away. I think he preferred her dark and bending.

I finish the rest of the drink, letting the spinning happiness ooze in. Then with a white rock, we sketch a little smile on the cup and name him Edward. We put Edward upside down on the cup stick with the rest of its red friends. We have sixteen cups now. I feel a little bad for piercing the cups through the face like that, but it's the only way to get them to stay together.

There's so much light coming through Momma's leaves. If she could bud flowers, I'm sure hers would be hot-pink.

I can't get too close though. There's a strange man sulking under her shade. He's carving something into her trunk.

Fall

Can Liz come over for dinner?

You'd think by now Alex would give up asking. His girlfriend is the prettiest girl in school. Long black hair with neon '90s clips always framing her round face. But Dad doesn't care about that, so he always says no when he begs.

Why not?

We all know where this is going.

Kiddo, don't bother messing around with women. They're all the same. Nothin' but trouble.

I don't want to be a woman if it means Dad won't love me. When exactly does a girl become a woman, anyway?

I'm too scared to ask. Especially when Dad becomes hot and steaming like this. At least he makes it easy to tell. He goes out onto the porch to cool down, stretching the phone line as far as it will go without snapping off the wall, and looks toward town. He bites down on his thumb while making call after call. *Have you seen her?*

అ

Mom's hair is falling out. The sidewalk is filled with her. I pick up as many leaves as I can, careful not to crack and break their fragile foliage.

I try telling Alex and Baby about the leaves, but ever since Momma disappeared, they don't talk much. I borrow a shoebox from Alex's closet and tuck Momma inside. I rush back to my room, but he catches up and watches as I open the box for one last look.

Why do you have a bunch of garbage in your closet?

It's Momma. I'm saving it for when she gets back.

He says I'm an idiot and goes back to his room. We're always in our rooms. Sometimes it feels like I'm the only one still alive in this house.

Winter

There's blood all over the bed and more still coming from between my legs. I scream and cry because I know this is how I'll die. Dad comes in and takes all the sheets and blankets to the laundry room. The only words he speaks are *Get in the bathroom and clean up.* I cry until Granny comes with a giant pink box. The cushions inside are soft like miniature clouds and she explains what's happening.

I cry harder; it's news worse than death. She dares to say, *It's not a big deal. Every girl becomes a woman in time.*

☙

The leaves on Momma's head are all gone, and the air is getting colder every day. Cinderella was always kind. But it's getting harder to walk past that liquor store to see Momma. She's beginning to become unrecognizable.

Now that she's barren of color, it's hard to tell that she's even Momma at all.

Where did all that light go?

I look around for signs of that strange man. But he has also vanished.

☙

Dad calls us to his special chair, the recliner in the living room that only he sits on. We wrap around him expecting a surprise.

She'll be moving back in. Just for a few weeks while she recovers.

The wind creeps in through the open front door. Her dead leaves blow onto the deck. Her shriveled roots plunge and twist into the basement next to an old mattress and some new suitcases.

Someone cut her down and chopped her up. She smells like sawdust. Her limbs are all hacked and void of that golden color I remember. There's a marking on her side that is fresh and red. A tattoo, Dad calls it.

We leave her in the basement, too scared to get close but wanting her near.

I go to my room and pull out my copy of *Collected Fairytales*. I flip to Cinderella's story. I reread the entire story but can't find the answer in the pages.

How do you mourn someone who isn't dead?

PLAYING PRETEND

Harmony Hazard

Somewhere in the clouds of my early memories, my mother and I sit on a rock. It is tea-time, the hour when the sun looks right at us in the season when everything turns copper, burnt red as rusted cans. My mother and I had walked into the woods where bark peeled in the thinnest of strips, silver light shattering through branches, and leaves rustled like old women unbuttoning their long coats with slow hands. There on the wet moss, we found the little boats of empty acorns, and now my mother pours tea in my tiny acorn cup. It is imaginary tea, but I don't see much of a difference yet. She teaches me how to take small sips, how to pour, how to toast: the etiquette of drinking. These are the first rules I learn about playing pretend.

I don't believe in bodies, I remember exclaiming as a teenager, while my friends rolled their eyes. I tried to explain that I wanted to own the adventure of my body, to make up its rules, that I didn't want to believe that the anatomy books knew more about what was inside of me than I did. *How do we really know?* I said, too excited. Back then, I was young enough to only think of bodies as metaphors. How quickly that ended.

Like many children, I was obsessed with magic. But I had a mother who was obsessed too. Magic wasn't making things float or disappear; it was something else: a belief system, a way of seeing, a way of finding.

As a child, I would hurtle out my window, squirm through a dense hedge, and plop myself on the neighbor's grass to pour sky into my mouth: a blue so deep it made me feel like I was fall-ing. It was below this sky that I first searched. What I was look-ing for could be explained as god or spirit or meaning, but what I found instead one afternoon, when I walked through the yard and peered into the bottom of the neighbor's rain-gutter, was a tiny bell. A gold thing I kept for years and jangled whenever I needed some luck, but like all lucky things, it was eventually lost. What was a bell doing at the bottom of a rain-gutter at my neighbor's house? That red-brick home, manicured yard, grand piano in the window. There shouldn't have been any small bells, not any magic, but still, there it was. Proof.

My mother tells me that when she was six, she was invited to sing on the radio. She desperately wanted to do it, but her par-ents thought it meant inviting too much ballyhoo for a little girl, so they refused to let her sing. Soon after, she developed diph-theria. This is how she tells the story, as if the lack of voice led to her illness, as if illness was something that she brought upon herself. She remembers getting shots, sipping water through a straw. She tells me that because it was hard for her to talk, this was when her spiritual awareness began. In the periphery of death, lying there, gazing at the ceiling until it cracked open for her and began to offer visions. She didn't know then that she would forever hunger for this feeling of ocean, this way of being lost and then found, and that this desire would lead her to drugs and sex and the Amazon. Once she had survived the sickness, she felt that she had healing powers.

You have to go through the bad, she says, *to come out as a healer on the other side.*

When I was diagnosed with breast cancer when I was twenty-nine, my mother decided she could save me. *You seem surrounded by caring people and mysterious Heavenly Forces,* my mother wrote to me after I had told her the news. *I am working quietly and*

persistently on the latter. On the day that I told her, she went to church and told the women my name. In unison, they repeated my name, their voices weaving a tapestry into the sky.

All mothers must want to save their children and most mothers must come to the wicked conclusion that they can't. But my mother believes too deeply.

My mother's spirituality is all encompassing. If I grew up with any religion, it was superstition: the alchemy of magic and belief. My mother opens a book and points to a word, or sees the rusty letters on a hotel as a sign, or keeps the crumbs from her dreams and puts them under a microscope under the clear light of the day. She meditates, drags smudge sticks throughout rooms, makes the sign of the cross with her fingers when a car makes a sharp turn. She uses Milagros, tarot cards, singing bowls, crystals. She will walk into any church, not caring what denomination, and when everyone stands to take communion, she joins them, and when they bow, even if she doesn't know why, she joins them, and when they sing, she sings with more stubborn joy than anyone else in the room.

I don't remember going to the doctor very often as a child. *Hospitals make you sick,* my mother loved to say. I remember lying in bed, holding some kind of inexplicable sadness, and my mother appearing at my bedside, sucking in the air above me, her hands swiping over my body, fingers curling above my chest, and then with a whooshing sound, she threw that imaginary pain behind her shoulder or to the ceiling, and spat it out. An excavation; a purification, a kind of pretend medicine that always seemed to work.

When I was a teenager, my mother gave me a book entitled *Creative Visualization.* As I lay in bed, I learned to visualize a pink bubble, into which I could pour my fears. Or I could imagine myself in a wild place: a field of tall grass, lazy knees, shards of light.

I had always been a daydreaming child. Because my sister was ten years older, I was often on my own, but I learned that as my parents ran errands, I could sit in a dark car in a suburban parking lot, nothing but miles of cold streetlights to look at, yet I could entertain myself by crawling through the labyrinthine, congested, trafficked pathways of my mind. I could go anywhere it seemed, and I did.

We only use ten percent of our brains, my mother often said. *The last frontier is in the mind.*

This is always how lonely children figure out how to feel less alone. But this new visualizing technique was different: this wasn't escape so much as protection.

But there was my mother the healer and then there was my mother who struggled with a kind of sickness for which she had her own kind of medicine.

During my childhood, my mother kept everything for art projects: the tomato sauce jars, scraps of wrapping paper, buttons that sprung off shirts, the broken plates perfect for a mosaic project that she would never get around to making. Everything waited for her hands, everything except for the bottles—the thick glass of fancy liquor, the travel-sized bottles she snuck onto airplanes, the wine leftover from parties—these disappeared quickly, as if my mother was indeed a magician.

My friend D. used to say, *Your mother knows to hide the bottles.* But one day while my mother was staying with my sister, my sister cleaned her bathroom and found a tall vodka bottle that my mother had tried to hide under the sink for furtive sips. You can't hide them all.

I learned as a child to always sniff my mother's water before drinking from it. *Grog,* I called her small glasses of liquor. *Goblets,* I called her large glasses of wine. I loved old words like

88

those, and I used them because they made the drinking seem like something benign, something from a fairy-tale. *Are you groggin'?* I asked my mother, laughing. Sometimes I forgot and called her *drunk* by mistake. *Tipsy*, she would say, correcting me.

Maybe all kids of alcoholics learn these rules for playing pretend. Pretend this doesn't scare you. Pretend you're still having fun. Pretend there isn't some secret sadness that fills your pockets and makes you want to drown.

In my early twenties, heartbreak led me into what I considered my Year of Saying Yes. Yes to cutting off all my hair; yes to sleeping with the car mechanic; yes to almost-daily yoga; yes to my first back-of-a-motorcycle ride; yes to whatever I thought could help. And so it wasn't surprising that one night, I decided to say yes to what helped my parents. I bought a bottle of whiskey at the liquor store before heading to a music show, taking swigs from the brown paper bag as I stood in the back of the crowd and the room swelled with song. This is the only time I can say that I nursed that bottle, or the bottle nursed me; I always forget who does the nursing. As the cheap gold liquid filled my mouth, I waited for the moment when I would feel better. It didn't come; not that night, and not for a long time. I wish I could say that I didn't become an alcoholic for other reasons, but it's just that it didn't work, and I couldn't pretend that it would. I was lonely and stayed lonely and that bottle only made it worse.

You can trace the origin of the word *alcohol* to the Arabic word *al-ghawl*, meaning *spirit*, which explains why the word *spirit* refers to the drink as well. My mother is then haunted by multiple kinds of spirits. But how can someone so spiritually aware be so dependent on booze?

You have to go through the bad to come out as a healer on the other side. But sometimes it seems my mother, the healer, is still going through the bad.

Now, as I lay shirtless on a table while someone pokes and prods me, I practice the visualizing technique my mother taught me. I am not here on this table; I am lying instead on grass. I am not in a doctor's sterile office; the sun is instead spilling across the sky, wind stirring my hair, an ant tickling my skin. There isn't a tunnel being drilled into my breast for a biopsy, there isn't a surgeon peering down at me with bad news; not a bag of chemo dripping into my arm, nor a radiation machine spinning above my head; I don't see the reflection of my bald head in the mirror; I don't hear the words of my boss: *Chemo got to you, didn't it?* There is only a golden field, pine-sap heavy in the air, my healthy body jumping into cold water, feeling nothing but alive.

The stories that my mother tells me about her time in the Amazon are part dream, part real: her memory and imagination churning together like the river tributaries that felt like home to her for years. Once, when my mother was staying in a Secoya community in Peru, she became sick with hepatitis from drinking the water. A healer brought her teas concocted from roots and sticks into which he had sung. As she lay in her hammock with her yellow skin, he shook a rattle made from dried leaves over her body, taking in a long breath to suck in her sickness and then spit it out. This was how my mother believes she was cured.

∿

I remember trying the energy healing technique with my first boyfriends. It felt intimate to hover my hands over them, more intimate than if I were just touching them. I didn't know what I was doing or what tradition it came from, but it felt like it worked.

I haven't tried it with myself. I don't know if I am a healer like my mother. *Thank your body*, my mother always said, years before cancer, years before I understood what could happen.

90

❧

When I was diagnosed, I thought that maybe cancer could finally be my pathway to god, to spiritual knowledge. Or maybe cancer would make me want to drink like my mother. I still don't know if I will come out, like my mother, as a healer on the other side.

What I do know is that I am no longer a child who believes in magic, and I can't not believe in bodies anymore. I have become an adult, resistant to any kind of faith, committed to my belief that the world unfurls without justice or order or sense. Yet I can't help but want to imagine that maybe my mother can save me—not with Milagros, prayer, or creative visualization—but simply with the stubbornness of her love. This reminder is the one small bell that I keep in my pocket to jangle in case I need to believe in luck.

What is the difference between imagination as survival and imagination as denial? My finite body and my infinite mind: this is all I've got to use.

❧

When my sister tries to talk to my mother about her mortality and her options for a death with integrity, my mother leans into me in her red flannel pajamas, with her hands suddenly so old, and whispers, *I'll just disappear.* Her plan is to get into a canoe and glide down the Amazon river like she did in her twenties. *I would tell you that I was leaving but then you wouldn't let me go,* she says, and I realize that despite dedicating years to spiritual knowledge, she is scared of dying.

My mother and I are doing the same thing. We are in parallel play, pretending together. She pretends she's not an alcoholic, that she's not going to die. I pretend I am not scared of both. Meanwhile, I am trying to imagine my old age: I am trying to believe I will get to have one.

I don't want to admit that I like the idea of my mother just disappearing. I like the idea of not having to see her on life support, not having to fight with my sister about whether we should let her drink goblets of margaritas on her deathbed. But my sister is more practical. *Mom can't just disappear,* she says.

Of course my sister is right. But still, I picture that boat. This is what my mother taught me to do: to visualize, to imagine, to pretend. This may be the only thing I can do: create this image of protection for my mother, for both of us.

So I picture that boat, seen from an inlet of land, as tiny and round as those acorn cups my mother and I once drank from, and I picture my mother waving to me, getting smaller and smaller until I am squinting, searching for her, but she has disappeared, over the waves.

PART THREE

RECLAMATIONS

RIVERS

Ariel Gore

I walked along the dry Santa Fe riverbed on my way to see the shaman. I'd booked the appointment even though it was $170, thinking it would be more efficient than therapy. One appointment would have to do the trick. As I walked, spring bunnies peeked out from behind lavender shrubs like we were in some old fashioned English fairy-tale. I thought about pink wallpaper.

❧

The shaman wore purple parachute pants.

I said, "I feel like a lot of crazy is coming out of the woodwork."

She said, "You need a cleansing. You need cleansing baths."

"All right," I agreed. My back hurt the way it always hurt. This constant companion of pain.

The shaman's golden goddess earring glinted in the sunlight. The air around us smelled like sage. She smiled, kind of apologetic. "Have you considered therapy?"

Everybody asks me that.

The shaman said, "I sense you have a dysregulated flight response."

"A dysregulated what?"

The shaman leaned in, lowered her voice. "I do spiritual healings, but you don't seem to have a spiritual imbalance. It's your inner child. Your childhood."

I shook my head. "My inner child? That sounds like it could take a long time."

The shaman folded her arms across her chest and sat back

in her faux-leather chair and laughed at that. "Yes," she agreed. "It might take a long time."

I tapped my heel. "Well, I've only got a couple of weeks to dedicate to this."

The shaman nodded, but her mouth still looked like it was laughing. "Did your parents ever act crazy?"

Why did we have to talk about my parents? I said, "Well, my dad struggles with schizophrenia and my mom had a bipolar diagnosis, so sometimes they acted what people call crazy."

The shaman nodded, matter of fact, reached under her chair, and produced a small drum.

"Maybe your power animals can help you. Have you had any sightings or dreams? Of special animals?"

I described the way that on my walk over, along the dry riverbed, little spring bunnies peeked their hellos. I told the shaman I'd dreamed of a happy raccoon dancing on my patio. I told her about my wife's stage-4 cancer, and the way I often dreamed of mountain lions and jaguars when the cancer spread. I told her about the deer woman who crashed through the glass window of the hospital in rural Italy and helped me after my daughter was born when I was nineteen; the same one who, a few years later, lured me into a tree trunk when I needed a pep talk. *Was this deer my power animal?* I liked the idea of having a deer as a power animal—from a kind of strength-in-vulnerability motif.

The shaman shook her head. "Have you considered the possibility the deer is you?"

I really hadn't.

&

The shaman played her drum fast and hypnotic and I had the sensation I was tracing a line, following something floating.

She swished her goddess earring. "What does your inner child want?"

I answered without thinking. "She wants to be alone."

And the shaman said, "That's right. Your inner child wants to be alone."

❧

My daughter was coming out to New Mexico, so I booked a week in a fifty-five-dollars-a-night pink motel spa in Truth or Consequences, three hours south, and then my daughter messaged to say she wasn't coming after all. Not right now, anyway.

My wife said it was fine if I went alone—took it as a writing retreat or whatever—so I drove the three hours, checked into the motel, headed up the main street toward the little grocery store to pick up something for dinner. Sitting on the pink-painted bench out on main street was Lola, this woman I used to live with when we were both young moms at Mills College three decades ago in Oakland. Now she's sitting on a pink bench in front of a window that announces: *Destiny's Keto Kitchen: We Cook. You Lose.*

Lola, wearing a pink furry hat and an orange satin slip, yelled at passing cars, "The money system is a scam!"

I waved. "Hey, Lola!"

She frowned and smiled at the same time and said, "Hey, it's you." And she shook her head. "I'm a hot mess, but I'm not a meth head. My skin's just bleeding because I'm a hot mess. I'm sorry I slept with that guy that you liked when we lived together." She looked down at her orange satin lap and started to roll a cigarette.

I said, "Don't worry about it, Lola. I'll always remember you as a good and loyal friend."

I didn't tell her I'd burned a photograph of her in the sink.

And Lola said, "We're fifty."

And I said, "Yeah, I'm fifty."

And Lola said, "Me too, girl. I just got sued by my landlady at the trailer park but her money system is a fraud. I told the puny judge, *I will not perjure myself in Zoom court.* But you can't say fuck to judges."

I said, "Yeah, they don't like that."

"Sit down next to me." Lola patted the wooden bench next to her. She said, "Oh my god, you just shrugged so Cancerian."

When we were twenty-three or twenty-five, Lola and I used to wake up early and take the bus down Broadway. We'd stencil the outside wall of the Alameda County family court building: *Misogyny: Look it Up, Stamp it Out.*

Now Lola lit her thin cigarette. She said, "Girl, I don't have any cash money, but I have rainbows and I have treasury notes and as soon as I get to Kansas, I'ma get my gold. I have the truth, see? But I ain't giving out pussy to get to Kansas. I got a secret for you."

I said, "Yeah?"

Lola cupped her hands around her mouth and yelled into the empty street, "Vaccinations are calibrated poison!"

Just then a woman with silver glitter eyeshadow opened the glass door of the keto restaurant behind us and I thought she was going to shoo Lola away for vagrancy, but she just said, "Lola, don't get in a car with anyone you don't know, all right? Just make that a rule."

Lola gestured between the woman and me, said, "Destiny, this is Ariel. Ariel, this is Destiny."

"Nice to meet you." Destiny smiled, and she nodded to us both and she said, "Be careful," and she ducked back into her restaurant.

I liked this Destiny. I said, "Lola, do you need anything?"

Lola shook her head. "Nah, girl, nah," she said. "Just remember I told you the money system is a fraud and the vaccine is calibrated poison. You heard it here first. I always was a journalist and a lawyer. I never needed a formal education, but I did get one." She licked her lips.

"I'll remember that," I agreed, and I slinked back toward the pink motel spa without any groceries. I climbed into an aqua-painted room which housed the shared hot springs baths, filled a concrete and tile tub with hot lithium spring water, and stripped off my T-shirt and jeans and stepped into the scorching water and scrubbed my skin and soaked until the water was cold. I dried off with a bright green towel and slipped my clothes back on and crept around the corner to my red room and locked myself in. I didn't go anywhere near Destiny's Keto Kitchen again, and I did like being alone there.

I did like being alone.

At home, my wife feels dizzy. She grips her skull and pukes all night.

At home, my wife rinses with steroids to try and make the mouth sores go away.

At home, my wife still wonders if she has a rib out or if it's the cancer eating away at her bones.

At home, my wife schedules a CT scan, then a bone scan.

I try and tell myself it's not awful of me to take my inner child to the pink spa motel for a week while my wife waits for her scans. I tell myself I'm storing up reserves. I feel tired all the time and I'm not even the one with cancer. I tell myself a lot of things.

"Where is your inner child now?" the shaman whispered as she beats her little drum.

I said, "Oh, she's alone. She has a tree house in the cypress on the beach in Carmel."

The shaman said, "What does she need in order to come back?"

I said, "Come back where?"

I'm in the tree house, wearing a red-and-orange-striped '70s T-shirt and pink bell bottoms. I'm safe here in my tree house. I look around at the unfinished walls, the view from the open window, out across the water.

"My inner child has her own beach house. Why would she want to come back?"

And the shaman said, "It's okay. She's not ready. It's okay."

I made an appointment with Bruce the Masseuse because he was the only bodyworker listed in town and open that week. He had five stars on the internet review site. Maybe there was only one review.

He gave me directions to his home studio.

I walked through the dusty streets from the pink spa motel, past O'Reilly's Auto Parts and the Circle K.

Outside a small stucco house with wooden statues of Native Americans and bears and a canoe and plastic dinosaur models behind the chain-link fence, a red and yellow handmade sign read *Bruce the Masseuse*. I thought, *These statues are kinda weird and racist.* But then I tried to put that out of my mind. What did I know about all the contexts of these statues and Bruce the Masseuse in Truth or Consequences? I said to myself, *Ariel, check your classism.*

"Ariel?" A thin Santa Claus man peered from around the corner of the house.

"Follow me back, Ariel." He smiled, making his cheeks brighten up, and he curled his finger.

I followed him around the perimeter of the house and in through a side door.

His studio had a brown shag carpet.

I stripped down to my underpants, got under the cowboy-boot printed sheet, stared up at a cottage-cheese ceiling, watched the slow fan spin.

When Bruce the Masseuse came back into the room he said, "Crying is common, Ariel. Crying is acceptable. Even sobbing. Everything is okay here."

I said, "Oh, thanks for saying," but I hoped I wouldn't sob.

I closed my eyes, then felt Bruce's hands at my throat. His touch was gentle, but I don't like strangers' hands on my throat when I'm laying naked under a cowboy-boot sheet in a house with wooden statues in the yard.

I breathed in quick. *Shit, I'm gonna get murdered by Bruce the Masseuse.*

Sometimes I read news stories about women who get murdered and all I can think is, *What possessed her to be there then? Didn't she know she was about to get murdered? I mean, didn't she know to run when she saw the wooden statues?* And it's at moments like this when I do know what possessed her. She thought, *I don't want to be rude.* Like you're literally going to give up your life to avoid seeming rude.

And then Bruce the Masseuse quickly moved his hands away from my vulnerable neck to my calloused knee and Bruce the Masseuse began to sob. And Bruce the Masseuse did not stop sobbing. At first, with each tear that landed on my skin, I flinched on the inside—wasn't a tear an intimate thing? But now Bruce the Masseuse grabbed my limbs like driftwood, and he kept on sobbing and clinging. Tears poured from his skull and I could feel the massage table I lay on begin lift up, like a half-inflated inner tube trying to float, and I patted the rising water on either side of me, and I wondered if Bruce the Masseuse could swim, but just then the door to the outside creaked open. Our rising studio-lake gave way and rushed out the door, and I locked eyes with a wooden bear statue—our savior. We scrambled into a wooden canoe and the wooden Native American statues animated into flesh, and we all shook off the wet as we careened down the river of tears that became the main street of Truth or Consequences, and we swept past my crazy old friend screaming, "The money system is a fraud!" and the street became a raging river that merged with the Rio Grande, and we each took a deep breath and we just kept on going.

SPAWNING GROUND

Gayle Brandeis

The tug home felt like nausea at first. A heaving. An upheaval.

The tug had been simmering inside me, an underground hum, one I could ignore even as it vibrated all my cells. Then my husband turned to me and said, "Wanna move to Chicago?"—the company he worked for was opening an office there—and the hum sharpened. Surged.

Chicago. Place of my birth.

I've described the tug as a homing device that went off in my chest. Once Michael said those words, it blared to life. I couldn't turn it off.

I'd left the Chicago area in 1986 to go to college on the West Coast. I'd always planned to return, but one thing after another kept me in California, then Nevada. I'd resigned myself to moving back "home" only after my death, when my family would pour my ashes into Lake Michigan per my request.

My natal waters.

Calling the tug a homing device felt wrong, I realized. That evoked a metal box in my chest, something with a switch, but this tug was not mechanical. This tug came from deep within my body, maybe deep within the earth. A magnet pulling me eastward. Homing instinct, not homing device.

I said the tug felt like nausea, but it felt good too. A welcome heaving. A happy upheaval.

Everything happened quickly once we made the decision—the tug pulled me through real estate listings until the right one shined like a beacon, helped me stuff our life into boxes. The tug yanked me eastward with such ferocity, I had trouble keeping my balance. I banged my thigh into a wall, hard, before we left; I watched the bruise change as we drove across country, going from blue and green to a dark, purplish red. It felt like a strange progression of color, a backward progression, but that felt right too.

I was going back.

As we got closer to Chicago, I could smell the lake even with the Jeep's windows closed. The tang of pondweed. Wet stone and damp sand. The scentscape of my childhood.

"Exit here," I told Michael, even though the GPS wanted us to stay on the freeway. I let my nose guide us east, the scent of the lake intensifying, the tug amplifying within me. I looked down at my thigh. The bruise had spread all the way down to my ankle. The texture of my leg looked different too. Shiny. Patterned with purplish red diamonds.

"Pull over," I said, my heart slowing even as excitement pulsed in my throat. "Now."

I jumped out of the car even before Michael could put it into park. I couldn't stop myself. I've never been able to run comfortably on sand—it's always felt like pushing against the current—but I ran faster than I ever have in my life.

The lake.
The lake!

I'd always been cautious getting into bodies of water, always eased myself in inch by inch, slowing at crotch, at belly, at nipple, but this time, I had no hesitation. I dove straight beneath the surface and the stones of my youth winked at me from the lake's sandy floor—the little pink ones with black and white spots, the shiny white ones with stripes of gold, the gray pocked ones I always imagined were fossils. The ache in my thigh deepened as my legs fused into one muscled length, my fect fanning to a finned tail. I flicked it and the tug broke open within me, flooding my whole body with relief. Gills slit open down my neck and water sluiced in, delicious, as I burrowed a nesting hole deep in the pebbly sand and wondered what I'd spawn before I died.

THE ORIGIN OF HER SUPERPOWERS

Sue William Silverman

One evening, the world lit by a moon the color of parchment, the girl walks past the town's swimming pool and finds a velvet worm. It's as if the worm wants to be noticed—donning a red and gold velvet robe just for her. The girl realizes that the worm has misunderstood: it can't drink from the chlorinated pool. It needs the girl to offer pure nourishment, and the girl needs the worm just as much, for reasons soon to be clear. She carries the worm home where she lives with her parents and sister. She builds a cage for it from bobby pins and hair spray. She places a soft cotton ball on the bottom, along with a thimbleful of water, and safely pops the worm inside.

On the girl's walk, she'd found other creatures she could have adopted: lice, cow sharks, horseshoe crabs, gray egrets, and crocodiles. All creatures millions of years old. All creatures who had already survived drought, fires, floods, blight, plagues, and pandemics.

The girl loves the velvet worm best.

The girl keeps it within easy reach, knowing she'll need it at a moment's notice. The worm tells the girl how its properties have developed over the course of 500 million years, with limbs on either side of its head that convert into slime guns. These twin streams of slime are used to immobilize prey. Once the slime touches the target, its chaotic protein hardens immediately and is always fatal. The worm feeds only at night.

Over the weeks, the girl studies the velvet worm. Turning on a small flashlight, she crouches beside her bed and watches how it maneuvers—its speed and precision—whenever a fly, spider, or mosquito enters its cage.

The worm is an excellent teacher. Finally, the girl is ready.

The next time the girl's father opens the door to her room late at night, when everyone else sleeps, she and the velvet worm move into position. How else to survive, to not go extinct?

Her own arms magically rise. They take aim. Shoot.

RECOLLECTING WATER

Rebecca Fish Ewan

This story would end differently had I known what puberty did to gills. How I had gills all along as a child, only to lose them to the hormonal exigencies of adolescence. I used to hate my parents for leaving me to figure out on my own how to breathe air. Not once before they left one-by-one—Mom when I was five, and Dad when I turned fifteen—did they mention that my differences were beyond those of an average dork girl.

At first, I didn't know water separated me from regular humans. I made up theories to explain why other kids knew how to breathe while I gagged on the playground. How their voices carried through the monkey bars—laughter and screams, high and happy sounds, a chorus of air. I'd open my mouth and drown in the silence. Air poured into me. I couldn't spit it out in any way that resembled words other people could hear. Inside my head, sounds echoed and rippled. My skull full of liquid.

My parents might have mentioned on their way out the door that I could've been a mermaid. That this was my potential.

And by mermaid, I don't mean half fish, half-busty woman, with long flowy hair, a shell bra, and no discernable vagina. No, not that. I mean an ocean woman, one hundred percent seawater. That could've been me.

Halfling fish girls, the wet dreams of sailors, make no sense. The ocean is too cold to survive as a hybrid human. But if I were made of seawater, the ocean temperature would feel perfect to me all the time, even under an arctic iceberg, temperature being a relative sensation. So says thermal physics.

I could have walked into the waves on any beach, dove under, activating my gills that, like training wheels for riding through liminal spaces, would've kept me alive until I dissolved.

But that's not the way life went. Instead I've tried to make one thing feel like another.

Air can touch like water, how it breezes across your arm hanging outside a car window. No, not that. More like how it holds you in suspension, adrift in solitude and quiet, when you sit alone in the backyard garden watching flowers bloom.

I'm still stewing about the missed opportunity my negligent parents robbed from me. Parents can be such a disappointment. Yet, how arid my childhood felt in their absence.

In truth, my whole life has been a drought response. Each day I learn a new way to need water less. I live in a desert now. I'm evaporating all the time. Skin and bones shrink away as I go about my days. I'm also a parent, so have gained a teensy bit of forgiveness and empathy toward my own parents' short-comings. Though I stuck around for my kids' entire childhoods, they still hate me a little for forgetting to tell them important information when they were growing up and their brains were still elastic with possibilities.

I have no idea what it is I forgot to mention to my children. How to fry an egg? Methods of radical self-love? How to acti-vate your gills before puberty? As a mom, I should've known whether or not my kids had mer-potential, but I didn't. I am a disappointment. I blame my husband, born miles from the ocean, whose veins flow with desert sand, for recessing the gill gene. Perhaps my children's changeling abilities incline toward other elements. I don't know what they'll become. This fills me with fear, doubt, and wonder.

Water is an incompressible element. No matter how hard you try, you can't squash it. Water won't relent, even if you don't know it's fighting back.

Puberty turned me into a swollen sack, all molecular ache and acne. And circumstance. The murder of a girl I loved like water changed me. I still think of how life would have flowed if that man hadn't cracked her skull. The day she died, we had begun to make up from an estrangement I conjured from my sense of otherness, jealous of how loved she was by people more human than me. She had been pure light. The darkness after her death rearranged all my cells. Sure, hormones moved things about too, but it was her death that condensed me most. I graduated from high school only sixty percent water and without gills. I couldn't even cry tears when my favorite teacher handed me my diploma and an oak sapling.

Water erodes whole mountains, given enough time. How it just keeps falling from the sky, streaming downhill towards the sea. My twenties felt like this. Constant wetting and wearing away. I thought I was growing up, pursuing what I felt I lacked. I was mistaken. I merely thirsted and searched the far horizons for a coming storm. I reveled in the promise of thunder.

As a child, whenever I could, I got wet. I splashed to school in gutters gorged with rain, walked under the shedding flow from shop awnings. I ran through sprinklers. Held tea parties in the deep end of any pool. Volunteered to wash dishes after dinner. Anything to feel water on my skin.

But water hasn't always been my friend. When I was five, a cousin tried to drown me in my grandmother's pool. I never learned why, but my life depended less on her reasons for holding me under than on my ability to hold my breath. All my underwater tea parties paid off. I lived. She was scolded on the pool deck and from that day forward glared at me. My life is full of stories of other people blaming me for the way they hurt me.

Still, I forgave the pool.

It's hard to know what you would have done given an option you never had. Had my parents told me more, would I have turned into seawater and drifted down the California coast, crashing as droplets on beaches while the current looped around the ocean? Perhaps. At least I would have finally visited Hawaii.

Though, perhaps not. Water must go with the flow. Who's to say I wouldn't have ended up in that patch of South Pacific sea so far from shore barely anything ever drops by to visit. Isolation gives it clarity. You can see for miles through the pure blue sea, but there's nothing to see. Yes, if I had become seawater, this would've been my fate, transparent and blue, with nary a plankton floating by to join me for tea. Just the quiet of still water, soft as air.

As life is today in the garden, only wetter.

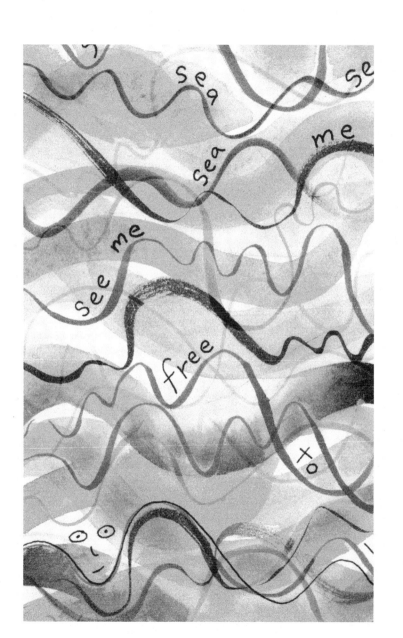

EL REGALO, THE GIFT

Alma Luz Villanueva

My final, fourth teen went off to university, and I moved to
Santa Fe/Holy Faith, New Mexico, from Santa Cruz, Califas. I
always lived in Califas—from Madre Mar to Madre Sierras. My
farm in Sonoma County where we—my familia and I—grew
almost all of our vegetables, chickens for eggs and meat, pigs,
and a steer I named Marty Burger, and ultimately could not eat.
Marty danced in the rain. My daughter Antoinette played her
flute at one end of the field when she came home from school.
Marty thundered to her; neither of us could eat him after he
was slaughtered. And I still very rarely eat beef. My cannibal
sons ate him with relish.

My youngest son, Jules, wasn't born during the farm years.
The final, fourth teen left for university, and my marriage of
twenty-four years was over. Off I went to Santa Fe/Holy Faith
to live alone for the first time in my life. I had been a daily
mother from the age of fifteen to fifty-five, forty years. I was
free to live my own life, just me, by myself. I dreamt a sacred
spot in New Mexico, a desert place with a high pinnacle rock
formation. To my right side, ancient rock paintings—hands,
hunters with bows, animals dancing (like Marty). I flew, in
dreams, to this sacred spot, so I could examine everything with
ease. When I moved to Madre Sierras, a dream led me there.
I had to reach my arms out painfully to a black dot in the dis-
tance, and expand it in spite of the pain in my arms and hands.
I saw where I was going—pine, cedar, a small field in front of
a cabin. I found it with my wolf dog, Zeke. I was pregnant with
Jules, then, but didn't know it yet.

And so, I found the high rock pinnacle while roaming
around. The instant I saw it, I felt the magnificent rock pin-

nacle praying. I expressed my gratitude in soft prayer—to my right the ancient rock paintings. The ancient hands, hunters with bows, the animals dancing. I knew I had arrived within my dream, milagros y gracias.

I wasn't used to this daily silence—no teens making loud jokes, loud laughter, Jules' surf buddies calling me *dude* as they met at our place to suit up, grab some snacks, and head out to surf Madre Mar. In the midst of forty years of daily mothering, I had imagined, longed for this freedom from time to time. Now at fifty-five, I finally had it, freedom, just me, my own thoughts as a poet, writer, woman—my own time, freedom. And I was unbearably sad every time I opened the door to my own, just me, apartment in Santa Fe/Holy Faith. No loud jokes, loud laughter, no *dude*. I wrote my poems of course, in this new silence. How I missed the racket, the *presence* and joy. My teens.

I secretly imagined a way to have a car accident, to leave my insurance to Jules, his unfolding life at nineteen. My beloved son, the youngest child. I was mourning my final, fourth teen gone; my twenty-four-year marriage gone. The marriage, it was time; I was done. But I had no idea how I would have to pull up each deep painful root of our life together—yet it was time. I went to the sacred pinnacle rock formation, the ancient rock paintings, at least once a week. A small, cold creek flowed by, and it was hot, so I sat by the creek, my feet in its soothing coldness. And I wrote some poemas—how I've always transformed mi vida. Y mis sueños, my dreams as guide.

I arrived in Santa Fe during monsoon season, the female rain like waterfalls, the male rain short gusts. Both welcome, the heat. One night I lay on my black leather sofa, a small reading light over my head, the room in darkness. A lightning storm blew in. The furious explosions, white lightning strikes across the dark skies for hours. I went outside to my small patio to watch and felt it shake my bones, my blood, my body. Back to the sofa, I lay outstretched, my feet in the darkness, a small pool of light over my head. Out to the patio to watch, to witness the jagged explosions, the bombs full of light, la luz. Back to the sofa, feet outstretched to darkness.

Then I *saw* it—a tiny, white, glowing lightning bolt entered my left foot. No pain. It simply slid into my left foot. A jolt of energy. I felt it traveling up the left side of my body slowly; I made myself breathe, and I fell asleep to the explosions of light, la luz.

I woke to silence and a sharp pain on my left side, mi corazøn. I breathed as slowly as possible. The sharp pain continued. I drove myself to the ER and was immediately hooked up to all kinds of medical gadgets. I made myself breathe slowly, slowly. I stayed the night. Toward dawn a young doc came into my room, looked at me directly, and said, "You're healthier than I am."

I laughed; he laughed. I drove myself home, back to my apartment, just me.

I sat in the silence and stillness on my black leather sofa. I imagined—*saw*—the tiny, glowing lightning bolt moving through my body. I realized it was moving through all of my chakras when it had gotten stuck in my heart chakra. Of course, my *heart chakra*, my mourning corazøn. I knew what I had to do, for the rest of mi vida. I had to learn to channel this tiny, glowing lightning bolt through all of my chakras. This regalo, this gift, of energy. And then I *heard it: LIVE. Shut up and LIVE! Start singing and LIVE! Start dancing and LIVE! Start traveling and LIVE!* I had always wanted to travel to Bali, and so I began the online search.

I bought a very cheap ticket to Bali months before 9/11. Bali was surrounded by the largest Muslim population in the world. Should I go or should I stay home during this turbulent time? I arrived in San Francisco—my childhood city—my connection to Taiwan, then to Bali. My tickets were canceled. I argued. I pleaded. I presented the proof of my tickets. A young Asian guy smiled, taking my proof, and within minutes he had corrected my tickets to Bali. He walked me to the gate just as boarding began and handed my ticket directly to the EVA agent. I was the only non-Asian on the half-full plane. I had four seats to myself—a bed with pillows, blanket. The beautiful female attendants welcomed us on board, hands together with a bow. Everyone returned the bow. This bow was repeated with all interactions. I loved this bow. Hot towels before eating wonderful food, refills of vino, cafecito, a pot of tea—the bow. The flights lasted over twenty hours, yet I landed in Denpasar, Bali, smiling and cared for. My tiny, glowing lightning bolt swam through my chakras, my dark sky. My mourning corazøn eased. *LIVE*. To arrive. Bali.

I arrived during The Great Celebration, which occurred every ten years, and coincided with my birthday—I was fifty-seven years old. During this celebration, all of Bali dances and sings, creating a wish for harmony in the village, the world, and the universe. I had no idea until I was given a brochure explaining this wonderful celebration.

On the streets Barongs—golden, rainbow dragon beings—with men inside, their feet exposed, danced down the streets to music, chanting and singing. An older man came up to me, welcoming me to Bali, nose-to-nose. An older woman, younger people, nose-to-nose, welcomed me to Bali. At first I pulled away, not used to nose-to-nose greetings—I began to cry, and they moved closer. And so I walked the streets, crying and sweating rivers in the heat. I had never cried in public before. I felt welcomed home, and I began to welcome the tears and the sweat, blending, cleansing. I was strangely home. I began to dream of my past lives in Bali—an island of dreamers.

I walked the back road of my hotel to avoid the crowds, and I could see the vividly green rice fields, a farmer waving, and the dirt road opening up to a main road. A long line of beautiful young to older women passed me, their lovely hips swaying, with tall offerings on their heads of fruits, foods, and other things I couldn't identify. I followed them to Pura Dalem Ubud Temple where two sweet grandfathers stopped me—I wasn't properly dressed. They smiled, speaking softly as they placed a white gauzy sarong around my hips, a black and white sash around my waist, and a white headband around my Ojo de Sueño, my Dream Eye. My Yaqui Mamacita had trained me in *dreaming* from the time I could speak.

A large group of men, with flowers behind their ears, were playing passionate gamelan. I heard the voices of women singing and followed the sound to a large courtyard filled with girls and women sitting on the floor. I had never heard this sound before, and I realized that the women were singing from their wombs. Beautiful offerings had been piled on the other side of the courtyard, and an offering that I would learn was the *Bagia*—an offering which contains all the contents and beings of the universe.

I sat plastered against a wall, a bare-breasted goddess, mouth open, above my head. I imagined roaring her song. Two visitors with cameras—a man and a woman—were escorted out by a huge Balinese man. I pressed tighter against the wall, willing myself invisible. The girls and women sang so beautifully from their wombs; I cried, of course. A lovely young woman turned to me, motioning me forward. My hand to my chest—*me?* She smiled, nodding *yes*. I scooted forward, joining the singing women. They raised flowers as they sang. I wished I had some flowers to raise. The women on both sides of me, gently smiling, gave me flowers.

A grandmother in her eighties, with long gray hair to her waist, reminded me of Mamacita, who, when alone with me, had also worn her hair down to her waist. This grandmother began to boss several teenage boys around, urging them to build a fire. A power radiated from her—no sweet, gentle grandmother! After the small fire began to burn, she took a large stick and scattered the fire. I realized the power of birth and death—my tiny lightning bolt danced in my womb. She began to circulate among us, holding a large metal bowl engraved with symbols, stopping before each woman and girl, to bless them with water. She came to me and met my eyes sternly. I raised my palms, gazing downward. I felt the coolness of water as the women and girls continued to sing from their wombs. I hummed, imagining my hum rising from my womb, where I had birthed four human beings now grown. I imagined my tiny, glowing lightning bolt singing with me. I no longer felt alone, as in lonely. I remembered reading this—*alone, all one.* "Gracias y milagros, Grandmother," I whispered.

A few days later I returned to Ubud Temple. There were no men with flowers behind their ears playing passionate gamelan, no women or girls singing from their wombs. I wandered through courtyards, passing below stone goddesses. I arrived in a courtyard with an eagle chained to a tall metal stand. I was shocked and outraged. An older woman approached me, radiating a calm beauty. I immediately asked, "Why is the eagle chained, not free?"

"What is freedom, madam?" she answered.

I had no response to her question in that moment. Instead, I asked again, "Why is the eagle chained?"

"If you join me for tea, I can explain." She motioned me toward her pavilion. I followed her, sitting on some lovely cushions in front of an ornate, wooden table.

"You see, this eagle is my ally in healing. She's fed and treated well for one full year, then I let her go. Yes, to be free," she said, with a smile, her accent lovely and fluid.

"Like a dream ally." I looked into her eyes; her gaze was pure will edged with compassion. I told her about Mamacita, a Yaqui curandera de Mexico who had taught me *dreaming.*

A young woman brought a tray of tea and sweet cakes, along with a beautifully carved wooden box.

The healer opened the box revealing exquisite amber jewelry. The young woman poured our tea. *What is freedom, madam?* Her question echoed in my mind, in my corazøn, in my womb. I would find many answers to this question over the course of the next twenty years.

When I wear my amber earrings, I hear her words, *This stone is the soul of the eagle.* Flight—freedom—to the heart of the Sixth Sun when my tiny, glowing lightning bolt returns to its source.

I gaze at my tattooed eagle, left hand. *What is freedom, madam?*

LEGACY

Diane Gottlieb

I leave my belly to the garden. May trees root in my flesh, flowers bloom in my soft, rounded skin. A shame I didn't appreciate how wonderful a place my belly was to grow.

To the ducks, the dear ducks I'd visit along my morning walks, I leave my sense of humor, my laugh, my own quirky quacks. The ducks. How I loved the ducks.

To the lizards, those dinosaurs who roam the lesser-traveled paths of South Florida, creatures from the past who'd take my breath away. To them, I leave my armor. It served me well, until it didn't. May they find a better use.

To my friends, my young friends, I leave my smile, the sparkle in my eyes. May they never lose theirs.

To my old friends, my oldest friends, I leave my secrets, the ones even they may not know.

I leave compassion to my second cousin—Lord knows she can use some!

My books, my beloveds, the hard-covered, the paper-backed, I leave those dog-eared, marked up treasures to my sister. May she swim with words of wonder, wade in waters of metaphor. May she only dare the thrillers before the sun goes down.

I leave my heart to my husband, who always held it so gently. May he take great comfort in its beat. May he one day give his own to another.

To my kids, I leave their memories of me. May those soften over time.

The bone, the sinew, the guts, the gore. I leave all these to my ghosts. To my mother, her mother before her, the women waiting in the wings. Drink me. Swallow me. Devour whatever's left. My shadow will join you in the haunt.

CONTRIBUTORS

Mare Berger is a singer-songwriter, pianist, teacher, writer, and gardener based in Brooklyn, New York. They have had two vignettes published in the *New York Times*. Mare's articles have been published in *Tom Tom Magazine*, their personal essays have been published in *The Body Is Not an Apology, JMWW Journal*, and a prose poem was published in **82 Review*. You can listen to Mare's music and read their writing at marielberger.com and follow them @maremoonsong.

Gayle Brandeis is the author of *Drawing Breath: Essays on Writing, the Body, and Loss*, as well as several books of nonfiction, fiction, and poetry. Learn more at gaylebrandeis.com.

Michaela Carter is the author of the novels *Leonora in the Morning Light* and *Further Out Than You Thought*. She is the co-founder of the Peregrine Book Company, an independent bookstore in Prescott, Arizona. Find out more at michaelacarter.com.

Laura Cline is a mother of daughters and teacher of composition. In her free time, she wears comfortable pants, does Pilates, thrifts treasures, naps, and writes words.

Christine Corrigan is the author of *Again: Surviving Cancer Twice with Love and Lists* (Koehler Books 2020). Christine gives voice to the beautiful ordinary in her lyrical and practical essays. Her work about family, writing, illness, and survivorship has appeared in anthologies, including *(Her)oics: Women's Lived Experiences During the COVID-19 Pandemic*, magazines, and other publications. Her essay "Relics to Reliquary" was recognized as notable in *Best American Essays 2022*. Learn more about Christine at christincshieldscorrigan.com.

Rebecca Fish Ewan is a poet/cartoonist whose books include the award-winning visual hybrid memoir *By the Forces of Gravity* and the cartooned craft book *Doodling for Writers*. Despite being born a fire sign, water tethers Rebecca to the earth and other human beings. She makes her home in the arid southwest where she lives like a hermit crab and university professor. IG: @doodlescriptorium

Amy Goldmacher is an anthropologist, a writer, and a book coach, which means her career has centered around transforming information for good. An excerpt from her flash memoir in the form of a glossary won the 2022 AWP Kurt Brown Prize in Creative Nonfiction. She is currently writing slightly surreal flash fiction and nonfiction. She can be found at amygoldmacher.com.

Ariel Gore is an award-winning editor and author of a dozen books of fiction and nonfiction including *The Wayward Writer* and *We Were Witches*. She teaches writing at literarykitchen.net. Gore thinks and sees the world in magical realism, and she feels most real when she can express her surrealist experience of the world.

Diane Gottlieb, MSW, MEd, MFA, is a writer and educator, whose words appear or are forthcoming in *River Teeth, HuffPost Personal, SmokeLong Quarterly, Barrelhouse, The Rumpus, Hippocampus,* and *100-Word Story,* among other literary journals and anthologies. She is the editor of *Awakenings: Stories of Body and Consciousness* (ELJ Editions 2023) and the Prose/CNF Editor of *Emerge Literary Journal.* You can find her at dianegottlieb.com and on FB, IG, and Twitter @DianeGotAuthor.

Harmony Hazard (@harmonyhazard) grew up in Tucson and New York, received her MFA from Stony Brook University, and has writing published in *Creative Nonfiction, The Rumpus, Catapult, River Teeth, Hippocampus, Essay Daily, CALYX,* and the anthology *Rebellious Mourning*. She edits nonfiction for *The Vida Review*, teaches writing full-time, and dreams of and from the desert.

Kara Hollowell lives and works in Seongnam, South Korea as an English Language Instructor. She is currently working toward her Master's in Creative Writing.

Rebecca Kuder's debut novel, *The Eight Mile Suspended Carnival*, was published by What Books Press, and her stories and essays have appeared in *Los Angeles Review of Books; Hags on Fire; Bayou Magazine; Year's Best Weird Fiction; The Rumpus; Crooked Houses;* and elsewhere. She lives in Yellow Springs, Ohio. Find her at rebeccakuder.com.

Leslie Lindsay's writing has been featured in *The Millions, The Rumpus, Hippocampus Magazine, The Smart Set, Brevity, The Florida Review, The Cincinnati Review, Essay Daily,* and *DIAGRAM*. Her work has been nominated for *Best American Short Stories*. She resides in Greater Chicago and is at work on a memoir excavating her mother's madness through fragments. She can be found @leslielindsay1 on X and Instagram where she shares thoughtful explorations and musings on literature, art, design, and nature.

Malia Márquez was born in New Mexico, grew up in New England, and lives in Los Angeles. Her award-winning first novel, *This Fierce Blood*, was published by Acre Books in 2021. Find her at maliamarquez.com.

Sue William Silverman's memoir, *How to Survive Death and Other Inconveniences,* won the Gold Star in *Foreword Reviews* Indie Book of the Year Award. Other books include *Love Sick: One Woman's Journey through Sexual Addiction,* made into a Lifetime TV movie; *Because I Remember Terror, Father, I Remember You,* which won the AWP Award; and *The Pat Boone Fan Club: My Life as a*

White Anglo Saxon Jew. She teaches at Vermont College of Fine Arts. Visit her at SueWilliamSilverman.com.

Deanne Stillman's books include *Blood Brothers* (starred review, *Kirkus Reviews*); *Desert Reckoning* (based on a *Rolling Stone* piece, Spur Award winner); *Mustang* (an *LA Times* "best book of the year," which launched conversations about wild horses in the West), and *Twentynine Palms* (an *LA Times* "best book of the year" that Hunter Thompson called "a strange and brilliant story by an important American writer"). Her essays have appeared in the *Los Angeles Review of Books* and various anthologies.

Alma Luz Villanueva is the author of four novels, most recently *Song of The Golden Scorpion*, and eight books of poetry, most recently *Gracias*. Her fiction, poetry, and essays have been published in many anthologies and textbooks. Visit almaluzvillanueva.com for more information.

ACKNOWLEDGEMENTS

No one becomes a writer in isolation, and no one creates a book of any kind alone.

I'm grateful to the incredible Chelsey Clammer for her help in crafting the proposal for *Becoming Real*. I am forever indebted to Jaynie Royal and Pam van Dyk for their tireless work bringing finely crafted literature to the global conversation through Regal House and Pact Press. My agent, Linda Roghaar, has been in my corner since 2000.

My father, Glenn Herring, Jr., first showed me the power of imagination. He wrote a little himself, though he never published, and he used the speculative to describe his experiences living with polio and then later heart disease. He taught me the value of different perspectives and how stories can connect us to what we don't understand or what we might fear.

All the contributors to this anthology were a dream to work with. I commend them on their willingness to share their experiences with me and the bravery and vulnerability it takes to put something on the page.

And to you, of course. Thanks for reading! The stories need us as much as we need them.

Here's to a wider, deeper, and more compassionate world.

Laraine Herring
April 2023

Book Club Questions

1. Which essay did you resonate with the most? Why?

2. Many of the authors dealt with grief in their essays and used a speculative device to help illuminate that feeling. If you were to write about a grief experience, what speculative elements might help you better share your grief with others?

3. Relationship fracturing is another theme in this collection, particularly the parent/child relationship. If you could embody any form imaginable to visit a relationship from your past that still has unfinished business, what would it be? What would you say? How might this encounter help heal you?

4. After reading the collection, have your thoughts on using speculative elements in nonfiction and memoir changed? If so, in what ways?

5. The speculative can be a great tool to help explore parts of our lived experiences that we can't put clearly into words. Did one or more of the essays help you see a way you might write into a complicated time in your life? If so, what technique or device from the essay helped?